# ACROSS AMERICA AND BACK

# ACROSS AMERICA AND BACK

*Retracing My Great-Grandparents'*
*Remarkable Journey*

Mary Ann Hooper

To Betty + Fred,

Happy reading !

Mary H. Hooper

▲▲ UNIVERSITY OF NEVADA PRESS  *Reno & Las Vegas*

University of Nevada Press | Reno, Nevada 89557 USA
www.unpress.nevada.edu
Copyright © 2018 by University of Nevada Press
All rights reserved
All photos courtesy of the author unless otherwise noted.
Cover photographs: (*background*) "Watson's new rail-road and distance map of the United States and Canada, 1871," courtesy of the Library of Congress; (*inset*) courtesy of Phil Richards.
Cover design by David Ter-Avaysan

Library of Congress Cataloging-in-Publication Data
Names: Hooper, Mary Ann, 1944– author.
Title: Across America and back : retracing my great grandparents' remarkable journey / by Mary Ann Hooper.
Description: Reno, NV : University of Nevada Press, [2017] | Includes index.
Identifiers: ISBN 978-1-943859-66-5 (pbk. : alk. paper) | ISBN 978-1-943859-67-2 (e-book) | LCCN 2017039502 (print) | LCCN 2017061399 (e-book)
Subjects: LCSH: United States—Description and travel. | West (U.S.)—Description and travel. | Railroad travel—United States. | Railroad travel—West (U.S.) | Rice, Charles, 1838–Travel—United States. | Rice, Fannie, 1844–Travel—United States. | Hooper, Mary Ann, 1944—Travel—United States. | United States—Social life and customs—1865–1918. | Brattleboro (Vt.)—Biography.
Classification: LCC E168 .H76 2017 (print) | LCC E168 (e-book) | DDC 917.304/932—dc23
LC record available at https://lccn.loc.gov/2017039502

The paper used in this book meets the requirements of American National Standard for Information Sciences—Permanence of Paper for Printed Library Materials, ANSI/NISO Z39.48-1992 (R2002).

First Printing

Manufactured in the United States of America

# CONTENTS

Preface ............................................................................................ *vii*

1 ❧ To Chicago: Destroyed by the Great Fire ........................... *3*

2 ❧ To Omaha: Gateway to the West ....................................... *21*

3 ❧ Across the Great Plains to the Rocky Mountains ............... *45*

4 ❧ Wyoming: Cowboy and Indian Country ............................ *61*

5 ❧ Salt Lake City and the Mormons ...................................... *83*

6 ❧ Across the Desert to San Francisco .................................. *102*

7 ❧ Arrival in San Francisco .................................................. *119*

8 ❧ An Excursion to Santa Barbara and Los Angeles .............. *139*

9 ❧ Back in San Francisco for the Chinese New Year ............. *161*

10 ❧ Return Home via Gold Mines and Yosemite Valley ........... *184*

Acknowledgments .............................................................. *203*

About the Author .............................................................. *205*

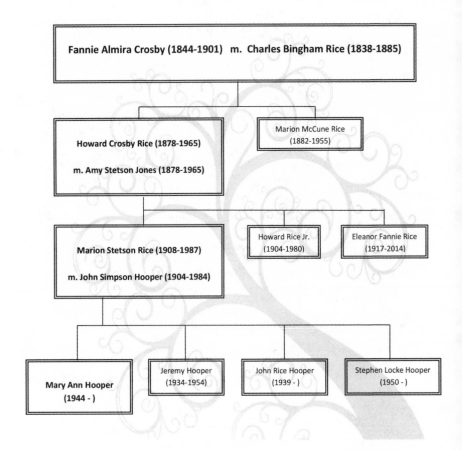

*My family tree, tracing my ancestry to my great-grandparents,*
*Charles and Fannie Rice, and including siblings in each generation.*

# PREFACE

WHEN WE PLAYED cowboys and Indians on the steep bank surrounded by hemlock trees behind our old farmhouse in Vermont, my favorite bit was getting shot and doing a dramatic death scene, crumpling down onto a mossy ledge with groans and gurgles and lying still for about ten seconds. We called it cowboys and Indians, but I don't remember any Indians, or any cowboys for that matter. It was more about law and order, with a sheriff and a posse and some outlaws, all of us riding pretend horses and shooting toy six-shooters. These games were usually with my big brother and his friends, and I was generally expected to raise my hands and surrender. I didn't mind. I would soon try to escape, galloping off on my imaginary steed, and then I would hear "bangbangyerdead!" and get to do the dramatic death scene again. Cowboys and Indians was a great game.

The excitement and fascination of the American West was an abiding theme while I was growing up in the late 1940s and 1950s. I was a voracious reader and loved history and biography, creating a vivid picture in my mind of intrepid explorers, vulnerable wagon trains, and fierce Indian foes. As a young woman visiting the empty, windswept site of Custer's Last Stand in Montana, I was struck by the fact that the battle happened in 1876, five years after my great-grandparents, Charles and Fannie Rice, went from Vermont to San Francisco and back by train.

Britain became my home as an adult and has significantly influenced me, but my British persona is grafted onto an American rootstock. By the time I reached my sixties, divorced from the Englishman I had married and recently retired from over thirty years working in British local government social services, I was happy with my life in Britain, but a road trip with British friends on Route 66, America's famous early highway, had whetted my appetite again for the

*Here I am in my cowboy costume, age nine, in 1953.*

American West. In Winslow, Arizona, we stopped at the recently restored hotel La Posada, which originally catered to travelers using the Southern Pacific Railroad. It reminded me of my great-grandparents' train journey. A fleeting picture appeared in my mind of a young couple hurtling across the prairies and mountains despite the dangers of the Wild West.

What was their journey like? Did they meet any cowboys or sheriffs? Or homesteaders? Were they afraid of being attacked by Indians? What did they do in San Francisco and California? It would be exciting to make the same journey as my great-grandparents and find out more about what happened back then.

I found an account of their trip in diaries handed down through my family, but the diaries raised lots of questions. Why was their commentary so unlike what I was expecting? I was surprised to read that they attended religious services several times a week, not just for their own and other Protestant denominations but also services for Jews, Chinese, Roman Catholics, and Mormons. Why were they prejudiced against American Indians and Mormons, but positive about the Chinese? Why was there no mention of cowboys? Why were Mexican Americans virtually invisible to them?

I discovered that trains still cover the route that my great-grandparents traveled, so I visited the United States in 2008 and spent three weeks retracing much of their 1871 train trip and California visit. I traveled alone, with a folding bike I had bought for transport in the cities where I stopped, packing my belongings in two panniers and a backpack. I had my first experience of traveling on American intercity trains, very different from nineteenth-century trains and also from today's trains in Europe. I met all sorts of people—from a homeopathic woman doctor whose ancestors walked the Cherokee Trail of Tears to a descendant of a prominent Santa Barbara Mexican American who was fighting for civil rights when Charles and Fannie visited.

I learned more about what sort of people my great-grandparents were and why they viewed the West as they did. I found myself dismantling the view of the West that I had held as a child and deepening my understanding of its past and present, while increasing my worries about its future. Join me on my journey of discovery.

# ACROSS AMERICA AND BACK

# TO CHICAGO: DESTROYED
# BY THE GREAT FIRE

*October 16, 1871. Slept at father's last night. Had an
early breakfast and went after to our house to pack up.
Got through in good time. Started in 8:40 A.M. train.*

—Fannie's diary

AFTER a day-and-a-half journey from their hometown of Brattle-boro, Charles and Fannie Rice approached Chicago with feelings of trepidation. It was the evening of October 17, 1871. Charles wrote, "We began to keep a sharp look out for tidings from Chicago, anxious to learn the prospects of obtaining lodging in the city that night. About seven o'clock we reached the outskirts and could smell the smoke from the ruins. As we left the cars, we could see the glare of the fires caused by the immense piles of coal still burning although eight days had elapsed since the great fire had ceased its ravages."

When I first read this, I was taken aback. I knew about the Great Chicago Fire from my school days, but I didn't know my great-grandparents had been there. I was reading Charles' diary because I wanted to repeat his and Fannie's journey through the fabled Wild West. When Charles wrote this, the couple had left their home in Brattle-boro, Vermont, the previous morning. Charles, tall and handsome, was thirty-three at the time. Fannie, her thick, curly, golden-brown hair pulled back from her strong-boned face, was twenty-seven. They had been married for five years. Still childless, and with a good income from Charles' partnership in his father-in-law's successful grain business, they had boarded the train to San Francisco, three thousand miles away, to see the wonders of the West. The transcontinental railroad, which had only been completed two years earlier, had transformed a tedious journey that used to take months by horse-drawn wagon or ship via Panama into a train ride that took as little as one week. Their route went through Chicago.

Leaving the train, they hired a hack to find a hotel. Shockingly, Briggs Hotel, which they had booked, was a burnt shell, but they learned that its services had been transferred to a building beyond the conflagration, so they made their way there. Charles wrote, "Passing among the ruins of the once stately buildings, we caught occasional glimpses of the moon peering down at us through the gaps and broken windows and great rents in the high ruined walls, not with a bright and silvery light, but dimly and darkly through the smoky atmosphere, as if the picture was too melancholy to warrant a cheerful light."

Their arrival in Chicago so soon after the historic fire reminded me that the Wild West wasn't the only thing happening in the United States at that time. The whole country was developing at breakneck speed. The railroad had reached Chicago in 1849 and, within twenty years, had become the metropolitan boundary between the settled East and the expanding West. Chicago was a booming city, with an ever-increasing influx of people, money, and goods. Its population had grown from 30,000 in 1850 to 330,000 in 1870, and it hummed with commercial activity.

Because wood was the commonest building material, city fires were painfully frequent in the nineteenth century. But Chicago's 1871 fire has become known as the Great Chicago Fire; it was the San Francisco earthquake of urban fires. Unlike most fires, which burnt down just a few blocks, this one was driven by a high wind from the southwest. The dire effects of the wind took almost everyone by surprise. The fire started in a barn on a Sunday night and wasn't put out until thirty-six hours later, on a Tuesday morning, by which time 300 people were dead, 100,000 were homeless, and the fabric and contents of houses, office buildings, theaters, churches, banks, hotels, and factories in the most built-up part of the city had been destroyed. Many eyewitness accounts were published afterward, and the most compelling were brought together in *Reminiscences of Chicago During the Great Fire* (1915). A couple of excerpts give a flavor of what it was like.

The flames, propelled by variable gusts of wind, seemed to pour down Randolph Street in a liquid torrent. Then . . . the fire was a mountain over our heads. The barrels of oil in Heath's store exploded with a sound like rattling musketry. The great north wall of the Nevada Hotel plunged inward with hardly a sound. . . . The Garden City House burned like a box of matches. . . . Toward the east and northeast we looked upon a surging ocean of flame. . . . (Joseph Chamberlin, a twenty-year-old reporter on the *Chicago Evening Post*)

We then hurried on toward the St. James Hotel, passing through some of the strangest and saddest scenes it has been my misfortune to witness. I saw a woman kneeling in the street with a crucifix held up before her and skirt of her dress burning while she prayed. We had barely passed before a runaway truck dashed her to the ground. . . . In this chaos were hundreds of children, wailing and crying for their parents. One little girl, in particular, I saw, whose golden hair was loose down her back and caught afire. She ran screaming past me, and somebody threw a glass of liquor upon her, which flared up and covered her with a blue flame. (Alexander Frear, a New York City politician who was visiting Chicago on business)

One of the burnt factories was owned by Riley Burdett from Brattleboro. He had been a partner in Brattleboro's Estey Organ Company and had moved to Chicago in 1865 to set up a branch there, but he fell out with Jacob Estey and established his own company. Charles and Fannie knew the Burdetts through the Centre Congregational Church—Charles and Riley were both deacons there. They had stayed with the Burdett family on a previous visit to Chicago.

After breakfast, the couple found their way to the site of the Burdett Organ Company, where Riley Burdett and several other Brattleboro people were sifting through the ruins but were surprisingly upbeat about the future. Burdett paused to ride with the Rices around the burnt area. They observed women and children searching for belongings in the rubble of their homes. Merchants had set up shop in vacant lots to try to sell off stock they had saved. Some people had even started to rebuild. All the mature trees were destroyed and tombstones in a cemetery had crumbled from the intense heat. Water was being sold on the street at eighty-five cents a glass (about fifteen dollars in today's money). Groups of poor homeless people huddled in whatever shelter they could find. Charles ended, "We were glad when the time came for us to leave the city, not caring to spend another night in that sad place." I felt lucky to read Charles and Fannie's first-person observations of that tragic and historic event. It brought that era of American history alive for me. I couldn't wait to repeat their journey, to compare the changes between their world and mine.

I was retracing their journey, but I had another goal: I was committed to doing my part to tackle climate change, caused by our dangerous use of fossil fuels. I had set myself the challenge of spending three months in the United States without renting a car, traveling only by train, bus, and bicycle. For this purpose, I had bought an American Bike Friday touring bike that can be folded up and carried as luggage. All my clothes and effects were in two cycle panniers and a backpack.

Charles and Fannie didn't record what luggage they took. They mentioned it only once, when it had to be weighed before they got on the train in Omaha and it was forty pounds over the limit, incurring a charge of three dollars and twenty cents (fifty-eight dollars in today's money). A contemporary account of the items considered necessary for women suggests what Fannie might have packed. In *Scribner's Monthly* magazine, Susan Coolidge, who traveled to California in 1873, provided a "practical guide for ladies." They didn't have to travel light in those days: the maximum weight for luggage was one hundred pounds per passenger. Coolidge wrote:

> "My advice to women therefore would be: provide yourself with a warm, substantial traveling dress, and take one other suit, silk or cashmere, something that will answer for the hotel dinner-table and for going about the city. This is all you will need, unless you carry letters of introduction and propose to see something of San Francisco society, in which case a handsome dinner or evening dress might be necessary. There will be warm days here and there, especially on the railroad coming home; and for these, half a dozen linen or cambric waists should be provided, to be put on at any moment when the heat becomes oppressive. You will also

6

want a thick outside wrap, plenty of thick boots and gloves, a hat with a brim to it, a relay of grenadine veils, and, by all means, an old water-proof cloak, to be used in stages or on horseback as a protection against dust."

I left Brattleboro in September 2008. I wasn't quite in my great-grandparents' actual tracks to start with—the daily train through Brattleboro going south was half an hour too late to connect with the daily train from Boston going west (through Springfield, Massachusetts, to Chicago), so I had to start by bus, from Brattleboro to Springfield.

I was feeling rather smug, with my minimal, lightweight luggage, and was ready to go. But before I left by bus, I felt I must visit the train station that Charles and Fannie had departed from 137 years ago. I wanted to get a flavor of their beginning and the excitement they must have felt. I found the old station from their time, still there beside the Connecticut River, but long boarded-up and awaiting possible restoration. I stood there and imagined Charles and Fannie looking across the wide, slow-flowing river to Mount Wantastiquet, 1,387 feet high and the mountain that dominates the town. Because much of its rocky, tree-covered flanks are too steep for building, it still looks exactly as it did when the couple was preparing to set off, with a hint of the coming autumn colors here and there. Gazing around their lovely New England landscape, they must have felt excited but also somewhat fearful to be embarking on such an adventure.

Some friends had asked me if I was worried about traveling alone on this trip. All I felt was excited anticipation, even when I arrived at the less romantic site of the Brattleboro bus station, located behind a smelly gas station on congested Putney Road and without the commanding view of Mount Wantastiquet. Whizzing down to Springfield on the Interstate 91 thruway by bus, I was delighted finally to be retracing my great-grandparents' journey, but I also planned to enjoy myself, to meet interesting people, and to see places I had never been to. I was keen to find out what it would be like to travel across America on the train and use my bicycle for getting around and exploring my stop-off places—I love traveling by bike. When I got off the bus at Springfield, which wasn't too far from the train station, I intended to assemble the folding bike, load on my gear, and cycle there. But time was tight, so I succumbed to the temptation to use one of the taxis sitting outside the bus station.

At last, I was finally boarding the transcontinental train. As I gazed out the window, waiting to start, I thought about what I knew of my great-grandparents from family stories I heard when I was growing up. Charles and Fannie were my mother's and my uncle's grandparents. As far back as I can remember, I knew that my great-grandfather Charles had fought in the American Civil War (1861-65). We were told that he was wounded in the First Battle of Bull Run, taken prisoner by the Confederates, and released in a prisoner exchange, and that he never fully recovered from his wounds, eventually dying at the young age of forty-seven. When I was at school, I enjoyed the cachet of being able to say that my great-grandfather fought in the Civil War. My younger brother, Steve, still has the musket ball that was taken out of Charles' leg. He also has the tintype of Charles taken just before he left Brattleboro for the war. My older brother, John, has the field knife that was issued to him. I remember being envious of my brothers, because all I had were some souvenir silver spoons that my mother gave me, which Fannie had brought back from this trip to the West.

We have since found out more about what happened to Charles at Bull Run. A corporal in Company C, Second Vermont Regiment Infantry Volunteers, Charles was wounded in the first two hours. The bullet taken from his leg was round, slightly smaller than the diameter of a quarter, and was left flattened on one side where it hit the bone. It suggests he was in close combat with an enemy soldier, who was probably staring down a long smoothbore musket and firing as he was charging forward. A senior officer on horseback helped Charles get to Studley Church, which was being used for Union casualties, but Charles ended up a prisoner at the end of the battle because the church was taken over by the Confederates. When Charles died, in 1885, Fannie continued to raise their children, Howard (age seven at the time) and Marion (age three). My grandfather, Howard, in autobiographical notes written when he was eighty, described Fannie. "My mother was an unusual woman—capable, courageous and strongly

*This tintype photo of Charles Bingham Rice was taken just before he left Brattleboro, Vermont, in May 1861 to fight in the Civil War.*

*This disintegrating note says, "Bullet which struck and shattered the bone of the leg of Charles Rice in the First Battle of Bull Run, July 21, 1861." The bullet was kept in the pouch. Now it is in the possession of Steve Hooper, Charles' great-grandson.*

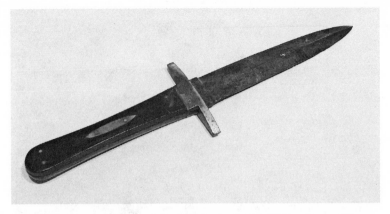

*This knife, probably issued to Charles in the Civil War along with a rifle, is a two-edged dagger, nine inches in length, with a five-inch blade. Now it is in the possession of John Hooper, Charles' great-grandson.*

religious. Her devotion to my father did not allow his death to wreck her life; she even refused to follow the prevailing custom of wearing 'widow's weeds.'" About his father, he wrote, "My only recollection of him is how he looked the day he died . . . not a happy picture for a youngster to have as a memento." When I read that, I felt so sad that my Grampa lost his father so completely when he was seven, without even some happy memories to hold onto.

The train I boarded for my trip was run by Amtrak, the main intercity passenger service in the United States. It was set up by the federal government in 1971 when private passenger services were rapidly closing down, mainly because of the postwar building of the interstate highway network. Services through Brattleboro closed in 1958 (I was fourteen) and didn't reopen under Amtrak until the early 1970s, after I had left home and was living in Britain. I am very familiar with British and European trains, but I can only recall two images of American train travel from my childhood in the 1950s—setting off on the train by myself, with my mother waving goodbye from the Brattleboro platform, and seats being made into beds in a Pullman sleeping car. I was looking forward to discovering what present-day American train travel was like.

Our train was called the Lake Shore Limited, reviving the name of a nineteenth-century route that went along Lake Erie. I had a thirty-day Rail Pass (469 dollars) for a coach seat. Charles paid 143 dollars apiece for his and Fannie's tickets to San Francisco, the equivalent of 2,350 dollars now—and that was just for one-way tickets, with sleeping berths extra.

I settled down in my seat, on my way to the West at last. I took out my journal to make some notes, but discovered I couldn't because the train was lurching about so much. We were also moving very slowly. I wondered if Amtrak was still using the trains and tracks it took over in the seventies, since the ones I'm used to in Europe are much more advanced. Then I remembered that Amtrak is federally funded and that trains are at the bottom of the national transportation agenda.

Our engine driver sounded the distinctive horn often—a long and then a short toot. Outside the window were the compact Massachusetts Berkshire Hills. Suddenly the woman next to me exclaimed, "Ye gads, a herd of buffalo!" I looked out at the grazing animals and laughed, saying my great grandparents hadn't mentioned buffalo until they got to Wyoming—and here they were in the East, grazing the Berkshire Hills.

Despite our slow speed, we arrived in Albany-Rensselaer an hour early, which just meant an even longer wait to get on the New York City to Chicago train. I wanted to visit Albany, the New York state capital, but although I asked around and looked at maps, I couldn't see any way to get across the half-mile-wide Hudson River on my bike without joining lots of fast vehicle traffic. I later learned that there is a separate pedestrian and cycle path on the bridge, which no one mentioned. I definitely would have used it.

In my three-month-long experiment in traveling with a bicycle and not a car, I was encouraged to find that the American car culture is facing some competition, especially in cities. Young Americans are buying fewer cars. Cities are beginning to allocate more space to bicycles. So much of American infrastructure was built for the car, rather than the horse, that streets and roads are big enough for sharing, unlike the old, densely built British towns and cities where finding room for bikes can be incredibly difficult. American pressure groups for better public transportation are also growing.

Cycling around rundown Rensselaer didn't appeal, so I explored the magnificent Rensselaer train station, the ninth busiest Amtrak station in the country. Built in 2002, it was the most modern station I visited in the United States. It even had visual displays giving instant information on changes in arrival and departure times, still not as common in the United States as in Europe. I was pleased, because I have partial hearing loss and can't follow the verbal announcements. Then I discovered, entirely by chance, that the visual displays were faulty, and my train was already boarding! So much for modern technology.

It seems that reliable arrival and departure displays for Amtrak trains are rare, but punctuality is reliably dreadful. The nickname for the Lake Shore Limited train service is the Late for Sure Limited. Train punctuality appeared to be much better in Charles and Fannie's time. They both recorded when their trains arrived and departed, no doubt using fashionable pocket watches on gold chains that were secured to their clothes so they couldn't be dropped. I have a handsome Swiss Tissot gold pocket watch that belonged to another of my great-grandmothers, and I can see that timekeeping would have been a bother, having to wind a watch every day. Yet their diaries say nothing about an even more baffling question confronting travelers back then—whose time? We take standard time zones for granted, knowing the time will move back an hour each time we cross a time zone boundary as we travel west. In 1871, time zones were unheard of. Every town set its own time based on the sun, so the correct time differed everywhere.

Conflicting answers to the question of the correct time have had lethal results for trains. In 1853, eighteen years before Charles and Fannie's trip, two New England trains crashed head-on, killing fourteen passengers, because the two guards had different local times on their watches. Companies agreed to set their times by specific station clocks so that this wouldn't happen again, which worked for a while. But the proliferation of railroads made telling the right time this way more and more difficult. The 1870 timetable for the Boston & Albany Railroad used by the Rices says, "Standard of time—Clock at the Springfield Station." From Albany to Buffalo, the timetable was on Albany Station time. But at Buffalo, served by several different railroads, the New York Central Railroad's time was twenty minutes ahead of Buffalo local time, and the Lake Shore Railroad's time was fifteen minutes behind.

Charles and Fannie got on the sleeper car at Rochester, so they were probably asleep when the train went past Buffalo's time-challenged clocks. It took another twenty years of ongoing railroad industry lobbying before international time zones were adopted. Although the Rices didn't record anything about timekeeping conventions, I'm sure they must have been a subject of conversation. The safety, or rather the danger, of train travel was something else they never mentioned, and I wanted to find out more.

After nearly missing it, I got on the Lake Shore Limited, grumbling to myself about the faulty display and the resulting problem for hearing-impaired customers. The coach car was more crowded than the one from Springfield, apparently because of the rising price of gas and the large number of people who regularly travel from New York City to Chicago. I noticed a woman in a uniform telling new passengers, rather officiously, where to sit. She wore a large badge saying Passenger Service Representative. Chronically cash-strapped Amtrak doesn't have computerized seat reservations, but makes sure they only sell enough tickets for the number of seats. The reps are responsible for getting passengers seated as quickly as possible, so they carry paper and pencil and scribble notes to leave on pairs of seats for use by passengers traveling together. I was struck by how old-fashioned the setup was.

My passenger rep didn't smile as she directed me to sit in a seat that was to be mine for the fifteen-hour overnight journey to Chicago. I sat down and chatted briefly with the ample woman squeezed in beside me, worrying about whether I would have enough room to get any sleep. I had not upgraded to a sleeper because it was much more expensive and because Amtrak's coach seats had looked fairly spacious, with a reclining back and a raised leg rest. I also wanted to meet other passengers. I turned on the overhead light to read—it didn't work. The rep was nowhere in sight, so I went to one of two empty seats she had marked with a scrap of paper saying "Schenectady," where the light worked, and started to read.

Sometime later the rep came along and asked me in an accusing voice why I was in a reserved seat. I explained, and said I would leave it when we got to Schenectady. When I asked her for an extra pillow she grumbled but said she would have a look. Then I noticed that she went back to my assigned seat to check the reading light. It felt like she was checking to see if I was telling the truth, not to make a note that the light needed fixing.

No one showed up for the seat at Schenectady, nor did the rep show up with any pillows. The train stopped at a station, where passengers were told they could get off for a stretch and a smoke. I got off for a stretch and started chatting to another rep, eventually asking him about pillows. He said, "You in the car with her?" looking towards my rep. I nodded, and he said, "Say no more. I'll get you some." So it wasn't me—she clearly had a reputation. Fortunately, she wasn't typical.

One of the things I like about train travel is being able to walk along the length of the train, so I wandered along this one to see what the refreshment car and sleepers were like. I had been surprised to learn that Charles and Fannie couldn't do this. Vestibules enabling safe transfers between cars hadn't been invented in their time, so it was too dangerous for passengers to cross the platform between the cars while a train was moving. Passengers were confined to one car and could only get into another one when the train stopped at a station and they could walk along the platform. Dining cars were very rare then, too. Long-distance trains actually stopped for half an hour three times a day so passengers could get off and buy a meal at a station restaurant. Walk-through trains with dining cars didn't start to appear until 1887. Charles and Fannie were seasoned rail travelers, so no doubt they packed their own food for the first day or so of the journey—probably canned meats, bread, and fresh fruit.

I found myself wondering about toilet facilities in those days. I knew they were provided on long-distance trains by the time Charles and Fannie traveled, but it is surprisingly hard to find out anything specific about them. Most of the extensive literature about early trains is aimed at aficionados (or "trainspotters"), so it focuses on locomotives and track building. I could only find two books published about the nineteenth-century American passenger rail car. One of them includes a drawing showing that a toilet on a train was a wooden box with a circular hole cut in the top, which opened onto the tracks like an old-fashioned privy. It was in a closet across the aisle from a small washing compartment.

Amazingly, I found out that dropping waste onto tracks still happens, and that this is only slowly changing in wealthier countries as rolling stock is upgraded. Some time ago, someone came up with verses for Dvořák's *Humoresque Number 7*, beginning:

> *Passengers will please refrain*
> *From flushing toilets while the train*
> *Is standing in the station. I love you . . .*

Unlike modern wags, Victorians were extremely discreet about such matters, but you can get an idea of what it must have been like from a contemporary account by Therese Yelverton, traveling in 1875. She wrote:

> Everyone is obliged to retire to rest at a certain hour and rise ditto, for all the beds must go up and come down together. Then follows waiting one's turn at the silver lavatory, which consists of two basins, a palatial roller-towel and a piece of soap. . . . I saw a lady take from her pocket a very handsome set of teeth, clean them carefully with the brush provided by the company, and place the teeth in her mouth . . .
>
> The lavatory is situated at the entrance of the car and cannot be made private either from without or within, and anything like a good wash is out of the question. You cannot even tuck up your hair or roll up your sleeves but some gentleman or conductor is sure to pounce upon you and remark, "Very refreshing to get a good wash."

Thinking how glad I was not to be traveling in 1871, I suddenly wondered if I *was* traveling in 1871: a group of pioneers had just gotten on the train. Coming into my car were women wearing plain blue dresses with pinafores and black bonnets. The men wore wide-brimmed felt hats, trousers with old-fashioned suspenders, and full beards. The children were dressed the same as the adults. Was I dreaming? I blinked, and realized they must be Amish. We were near Pennsylvania, the center of Amish country, and the Amish don't drive cars, but they do use trains. At all the stations on the way to Chicago, groups of Amish got off and others got on. The dress of each group was always slightly different from that of the previous group. I later read a book about the Amish, which said that the length of a woman's sleeves tells others where she is on an Amish continuum from conservative (longer) to liberal (a bit shorter). For men, it's the width of the brims on their hats.

I was lucky to have two seats still to spread out on, but I only slept sporadically. Early the next morning, I spotted a cowboy at the far end of the refreshment car, sporting a handlebar moustache, a Stetson hat, a paisley-patterned vest, and the obligatory cowboy boots. Maybe he had a job herding cattle, but more likely he was a type described as a "drugstore cowboy" or "all hat and no cattle," and just liked wearing the gear. Out the window beyond him was flat Ohio. It was nearly sunrise, which I rarely see, so I was pleased to be catching it. As the sun rose behind the train, a golden glow spread over the fields of wheat and corn. Tall silvery grain silos cast long shadows, and strands of glowing mist hovered above the fields. I relaxed and watched the passing scenery with satisfaction. Yes, I had left the East and I was heading in the right direction.

I was pleased that my decision not to rent a car was working out. I had decided a couple of years earlier that the threat we face from humans warming up the atmosphere by burning fossil fuels was the number-one issue we must deal with. I've always had a social conscience, a product of my upbringing, and have worked for social justice, joining various campaigns as they came along, but this one was different, broader, affecting everyone. I joined Friends of the Earth, I marched to demand action on climate change, and I decided I had better reduce my own carbon footprint—use less fossil fuel, stop flying . . .

Hmmm, that wasn't going to be so easy, living three thousand miles across an ocean from my home country. I investigated traveling by freighter, but it would take about three weeks and cost three times more than a flight. I compromised and chose to forsake the car instead. It was a start.

I wondered about whether Charles and Fannie had social consciences. I believe they did, but they showed theirs in church involvement. They gave significant time and effort to being teachers for Sunday School, which many people attended to learn how to read and write, possibly more than to learn the gospel.

A question that wasn't answered by any of the diaries was why the Rices undertook this long journey in 1871. On the day they departed, Charles wrote: "The last goodbyes having been said, we left home wondering how long we should be gone, how and when we should return." That sounded decidedly open-ended and adventurous. Were they considering not returning? Charles didn't seem to be close to his own family, but Fannie was. I can't imagine her considering moving so far away. Charles' employer/partner was his father-in-law, so time off work was probably easily negotiated and expenses perhaps subsidized or paid for. Were they looking for treatment for Charles' wounds, his damaged leg that kept getting infected? He did visit and bathe in a few hot springs on the trip, but only occasionally. It had been five years since they married, and no children had arrived. Were they hoping a long vacation might change this? Who knows?

Perhaps a trip out West simply took their fancy. It was only two years since the transcontinental railroad had made the trip practical for tourists. The couple's diaries show that they liked traveling, having gone on several substantial trips since they were married. Their love of traveling appealed to me as the reason, because I love traveling, too. It felt good to know we shared this affinity for going out in the world and exploring new landscapes. But none of the diaries give any more indication of the reason for the trip, so I am just guessing. We don't know. Of course they did return home, but not until May of the following year, nearly seven months later.

Soon enough my train arrived at Chicago's Union Station, one of the few classic, still-operational American train stations built in the heyday of railroads. (It wasn't burned down when Charles and Fannie visited because it wasn't built until 1925.) I made my way through the large high-ceilinged Great Hall, with its marble walls and Corinthian columns, and went outside to get a glimpse of the modern Chicago that I had visited in the 1980s. The sea of shining skyscrapers was such a complete contrast to the charred city ruins that Charles and Fannie looked out on that I had to pause and remember their stark descriptions. Then I went back into the station to look for the commuter train that went to Burr Ridge, about twenty miles southwest in the city outskirts, where I would spend the next forty-eight hours with my sister-in-law's family.

I planned to research the 1870s West by visiting local libraries during my trip, but I drastically underestimated the time that would require. If I had planned better, I would have gotten a rail pass that lasted more than thirty days. In Chicago, I managed only two library hours. My sister-in-law's brother Jerry commuted by car to work, so he drove me into Chicago and reluctantly left me and my bike on a street (that he said used to be an Indian trail), expressing concern about the dangers of cycling. But it was no worse than the British city cycling I was used to, so I wasn't fazed. I even found a cycle lane through the University of Illinois and most of the way to Union Station, where I stored my panniers in a locker and continued cycling to the shore of Lake Michigan, one of the five Great Lakes that form the largest freshwater system on Earth.

I turned north onto the Chicago Lakefront Trail, a full-on cycle highway—wide, surfaced, and with a yellow line down the middle and two lanes. It swooped around and onto a bridge, up over a street, and then alongside and underneath the four-lane Lake Shore Drive, with towering skyscrapers on the city side and beaches on the lake side. The contrast between the sharp edges of the Chicago cityscape and the lake extending like a smooth sea to an empty horizon was striking. I shared five miles of the trail with walkers, roller skaters, other cyclists, and even a police car, enjoying the peaceful urban lake side on my way to the Chicago History Museum.

*I explore the Chicago Lakeside Trail on my way to the History Museum.*

There, I browsed among the substantial material about the Chicago Fire, finding the eyewitness accounts that were so much more detailed than the descriptions in Charles and Fannie's diaries. It brought home to me the horrors of that time and what it must have been like. Too soon, I had to leave the museum to return to the station. Emerging into steady rain and a gloomier view of Chicago than when I arrived, I remembered with a sinking heart that I had left my rain gear in the locker at the station. But to my amazement and delight, buses were going by with bike racks on the front. Bike racks! On buses! Nothing like that in Britain. A passerby even kindly showed me how to operate one. I returned to Union Station without getting wet, ready to board the California Zephyr for the next stage of my trip.

My great-grandparents left behind the comforts and certainties of their small town in rural Vermont to begin their Grand Tour of the American West, and on the second day of their journey, had to deal with the heartbreaking sight of a major disaster in Chicago and its effect on their own friends' livelihoods. After their dispiriting day, they left as soon as possible, stopping for the night in the town of Wheaton, just thirty miles from the city. They joined in an upbeat conversation with fellow travelers over dinner, which seemed to raise their spirits and provide welcome relief. Perhaps it gave them the confidence to believe that any other adventures ahead would be more positive.

I had begun my trip, repeating their trip, on a train that felt, from my British perspective, like it should be in a museum, a startling refutation of the common European assumption that everything in America is bigger, better, and more up to date. But I had also enjoyed seeing the wide-open views of the country from a train, had observed various quirky people, and had established that traveling by train with my bike was going to work. Clearly the old-fashioned trains were still up to the job. We had surmounted the first hurdles of our epic trips, the Rices and I. Nothing could stop us now.

# TO OMAHA:
# GATEWAY TO THE WEST

*October 19, 1871. Left Wheaton at 9:30 a.m. for Dixon
where we are to take the Pacific Express for Omaha. Geneva
on the Fox River thirty-six miles from Chicago is a fine place.
The country along the Rock River is beautiful, all along
are such beautiful building sites and the land so fine.*
—Charles' diary

My delight at the bus bike racks and staying dry evaporated rapidly when I arrived at the Amtrak station and was told I was too late to check the bike in as luggage. I was used to boarding trains in Britain at the last minute with luggage and bike, and didn't realize I was supposed to arrive at least forty-five minutes before departure to check in. I looked for a trolley—none provided. I asked for a Red Cap porter—all busy. I was expected to get my backpack, two loaded panniers, and the bag containing twenty-five pounds of bike onto the train myself. I struggled along the platform—American trains are *big* and they go on forever—until another passenger took pity on me, carried the panniers, and helped me lift the bike bag onto the train. Relieved that the ordeal was over, I resolved that next time I'd get to the station well ahead of time.

From Chicago, it was five hundred miles to Omaha across flat Illinois, over the Mississippi River, and across even flatter Iowa—through terrain made up of vast glacial deposits that became grassland prairie in the semi-arid climate after the ice retreated. In 1871, this fertile land was being homesteaded and was becoming America's corn and wheat belt. Charles noted the attractions of the Western states, if he was to take up farming.

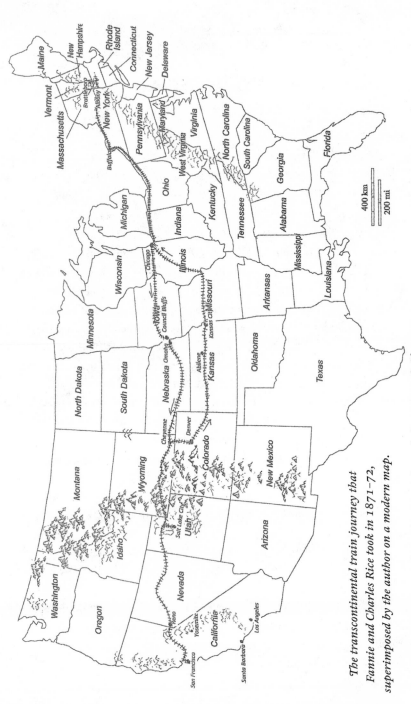

The transcontinental train journey that
Fannie and Charles Rice took in 1871–72,
superimposed by the author on a modern map.

Courtesy of D-Maps.com, http://d-maps.com/carte.php?num_car=5185&lang=en.

This leg of the journey took nine hours compared to twenty-four hours for the Rices, and followed a route to the south of theirs. There were several lines built westward from Chicago in the 1860s, when companies were competing for business, but almost all are now closed. Amtrak's present-day California Zephyr route was named after an earlier route of that name, which was launched with snappy upmarket fanfare in 1949, with boasts about the train's five Vista Dome cars and four sleeping cars. Just twenty years later, it was mothballed because people were no longer using trains.

Its modern namesake wasn't as luxurious, but I was delighted that the California Zephyr had two levels and that one of the cars included an Observation Lounge on top, based on the Vista Domes of the train's earlier incarnation. Long seats on each side faced outward toward glass dome windows and panoramic views. I had never experienced a train carriage designed for tourists. I found a seat, looked out, and saw flat fields of crops spread out to the distant horizon on all sides. Charles described exactly the same view. It certainly was panoramic, but it hardly changed, and it went on and on and on some more. For Charles it was completely new, so perhaps he didn't get bored, but I did, and my thoughts strayed to my childhood impressions of the American West.

I was born in 1944, so radio gave me my first taste of popular culture. I would sit on the living room carpet in front of the speaker, listening raptly to *Our Miss Brooks*, *Amos 'n' Andy*, *Roy Rogers*, and *Gene Autry*, but my favorite show was *The Lone Ranger*. I can still hear the stirring theme, the *William Tell Overture*; the sounds of a horse galloping; and the call of "Hi-Yo Silver, away!" Then the announcer intoned, "With his faithful Indian companion, Tonto, the daring and resourceful masked rider of the Plains led the fight for law and order in the early West. Return with us now to those thrilling days of yesteryear. The Lone Ranger rides again!" And gruff Tonto: "That right, Kemosabe."

Our family didn't go to the movies much, so after radio, television was our medium. We didn't get a television until 1957, when I was thirteen, but I occasionally managed to watch the black-and-white set belonging to our neighbors just up the road. I remember seeing *The*

*The California Zephyr's Observation Lounge car offers a panoramic view of the passing scenery. Here we are approaching Omaha.*

*Life and Legend of Wyatt Earp.* Based on the life of a real marshal, it felt like real history. *Bonanza*, the series about the Cartwright family on the Ponderosa Ranch in 1860s Nevada, came along soon after (and I was still watching it with my sons in the 1970s). Because it was about a ranching family, it also felt like it was based on real history. Although the cowboy is the traditional image of the frontier westerner, as far as I can remember only *Bonanza* featured cattle ranching. All the other shows were about establishing "law and order" in small western frontier towns, with the main character being a marshal or a sheriff.

In the years after I grew out of playing cowboys and Indians, I was given books about the history of the American West that I devoured with enthusiasm. They were in my old bookcase when I was clearing it after my parents died, and because those books felt like such an important part of my childhood, I shipped them back to Britain, along with some prints of cowboy and Indian scenes painted by Charles Russell and Frederick Remington. I dug the books out when I started planning this trip.

The earliest one, *Pictorial History of the Wild West* (1954), has a drawing of a revolver on the cover and a tagline that says, "A true account of the bad men, desperadoes, rustlers, and outlaws of the old West—and the men who fought them to establish law and order." It is a history of the period between the Civil War and the end of the century, when the rule of law was being established. Despite its claim to objectivity, it repeats many legends without checking the facts and is steeped in nostalgia for an earlier, allegedly more heroic, time.

When I started catching up on the history of the West in preparation for this trip, I found a book by Patricia Limerick called *The Legacy of Conquest: The Unbroken Past of the American West* (1987). Her interpretation was a revelation to me. First, she described what she called the American origin myth or creation myth, a theory about the significance of the frontier formulated by the famous historian Frederick Jackson Turner toward the end of the nineteenth century. The creation myth said that, in contrast to that of Europe, North America's land was available for the taking. Hardy pioneers gradually extended the frontier, replacing savagery with civilization and creating a new nation and a new national character based on individualism, self-reliance, and simple democracy.

Limerick pointed out that this frontier story was told from the ethnocentric viewpoint of white Americans, and she proposed a new organizing idea to replace it: "The history of the West is a study of a place undergoing conquest and never fully escaping its consequences . . . " She described it as a meeting ground for Indian America, Latin America, Anglo-America, Afro-America, and Asia, in which the workings of conquest tied these diverse groups into a single story about deciding ownership of the land, the effects of which continue to this day.

Limerick's explanation chimed with my present-day understanding of the role in world history of conflict between different cultures and races. I looked at another of my treasured childhood books with fresh eyes, realizing that *The Book of the American West* (1963) was not as comprehensive as it claimed, but rather ethnocentric, telling the "taming" of the West from a white male perspective and ignoring the story from other points of view. I started reading more books to fill the many gaps in my knowledge—and now I was on my way to the place where it all actually happened.

My train arrived at the Mississippi River, the chief river of the largest water drainage system in North America, and we crossed into the Iowa city of Burlington, south of the Rices' crossing from Fulton, Illinois, to Clinton, Iowa. Burlington didn't impress me the way Fulton and Clinton had impressed Charles, but the mighty Mississippi River and the long bridge stretching across its incredible width were wonderful. I marveled as the train rumbled for half a mile through seven huge iron trusses, with the stately river beneath. I might also have held my breath if I had known that five fully loaded barges had crashed into this bridge during a recent flood, causing so much damage that the bridge had to be rebuilt!

Night soon fell, so I could see nothing outside: no more flat fields stretching to the horizon. I listened for a while to a loquacious young woman in tight jeans, with electric pink hair and rose-tinted spectacles, who was chattering away to all and sundry about her motorcycle and Texas. Then her voice faded away and I found myself thinking about my saga with Fannie's diaries.

When I first started looking at my great-grandparents' diaries for 1871–72, I was disappointed to find that Fannie's for 1871 and some other years were missing. I knew that they had been in my uncle's possession, because he kept meticulous records that I had checked. Where had they gone? I spent many months inquiring of my family and local history buffs, but with no luck.

To my astonishment, they turned up unexpectedly just five days before this trip. My cousin Michel Chalufour was sorting out his aunt's papers, though it had been several years since she died, and had started on a box labeled with her initials, F. C. R. (for France Chalufour Rice). Inside he found the diaries of another F. C. R., Fannie Crosby Rice. France Rice's husband was Fannie's grandson and my late uncle, the custodian of Fannie's and Charles' diaries. The two women having the same initials must have caused the mix-up. Michel contacted my brother, who contacted me.

Thanks to more incredible good luck, the diaries were surprisingly convenient to collect, despite my self-imposed restriction to public transportation and a bicycle. Michel's son Marc worked in Boston and, two days before the start of my trip, I happened to be passing through on my way by train from Maine to Boston, and back to Vermont by bus. I cycled to a meeting place on the steps of Trinity Church in Copley Square and Marc handed them over to me. What serendipity!

As soon as I was on the bus to Vermont, I looked for Fannie's diaries for 1871 and 1872. Her diary for 1872 was still missing, but her 1871 diary was there, with a handsome embossed green leather cover and a clever built-in clasp holding it shut. Under the clasp, my fingers revealed a strip of embossed red leather and a pocket with something inside. I carefully slid out a piece of folded paper with "Mrs. Rice" written on it in faded brown ink. Inside was a curl of pale blond hair and the words "a lock of hair from my youngest, for Mrs. Rice." It wasn't signed. In another pocket at the back of the diary I found a letter dated the day before the Rices' departure, which ended, "I am so selfish as to hope you will both get tired of travelling and come home in 3 months, not that I expect you will. Write me often. May our Father protect you in the earnest prayer of your friend, Helen M. Howard." Underneath, in pencil, was written "Amen," probably by Fannie. Fannie's diaries showed that Helen Howard was a close friend and that they corresponded regularly when Fannie was traveling. The keepsake locket of hair may have been taken from Helen's daughter, but I can't be sure.

The material and construction of the diary were beautiful, but it was also tiny, and my heart sank. Each page was for three days, just one inch per day, room for only the briefest entry, in miniscule writing. I had been hoping that she wrote more than Charles did about practical things, such as what the trains were like. Though her entries were sparse, they did sometimes add a different perspective, and even without her diary for 1872, they made a worthwhile contribution, giving me a flavor of her take on things.

Charles left a lot more in writing about the trip. In 1871 he had kept his usual diary (one page a day), and expanded on his entries almost daily in a separate loose-leaf notebook that he continued into 1872. He also wrote about the trip in a small leather-bound notebook, possibly later when he was back home. His diary for 1871 includes numerous unidentified pressed wildflowers which don't appear in any other diaries, so they were probably collected on the trip. I like to imagine the two of them finding wildflowers they had never seen before, and Charles tucking them between the pages of his diary.

———

MY TRAIN TO OMAHA, unlike the one in Massachusetts or Charles and Fannie's, ran smoothly on good tracks and I could even write in my diary. I was already a thousand miles from Brattleboro, but I was impatient to put the flat part of the country behind me. I had driven across it on earlier trips at sixty miles per hour, which felt pretty slow, and our California Zephyr's average speed was only forty mph. (British trains go over 100 mph.) I know that people routinely use fossil-fuel-guzzling airplanes to cross the expanse of our large country, and I wish that Americans would embrace high-speed rail (over 125 mph), which is far better environmentally than airplanes. When I struck up a conversation with the helpful young man who had carried my panniers, I was delighted to find a kindred spirit. He was earning a distance learning master's degree in environmental studies at Antioch University New England, and was traveling by train to avoid flying. We shared information about the benefits of public transportation. I was surprised to learn from him that 98 percent of Americans have never been on an intercity train, but I had forgotten how sparse train services are in America these days.

Unlike me, Charles and Fannie had to spend a night on the train before reaching Omaha. Early the next morning, they saw another Brattleboro friend, who used to work for Estey & Wyman's mill. Dan (they didn't give his surname) met them at the train station in Dunlap, Iowa, where they stopped for breakfast. They must have arranged the meeting by telegram. I found a newspaper story from 1870 that describes a transcontinental train journey in which a telegram was dispatched home to inquire about the health of a wife, and an answer came after only forty-seven further miles. So the telegraph was almost as immediate as texting—but a lot more expensive, and only available to the well-off.

At 9:30 A.M., the Rices arrived in Council Bluffs, Iowa, on the east bank of the Missouri River, checked into the Ogden Hotel, and went to bed. Something they ate the previous evening had upset their stomachs, but in a few hours they felt better and went for a stroll around the city. Charles remarked, "The morals of this town rank above the average of western towns." I wonder how he was so sure of that. In the evening they visited Laban Childs, probably someone else from Brattleboro, and the next day went to visit friends on the Omaha side of the Missouri River. From Council Bluffs, the railroad bridge across the river wasn't yet finished, so travelers used a ferry.

The Rices were visiting Mr. and Mrs. Truman Buck. After finding that the Bucks were "pleasantly situated," they all went for a walk to see the high school that had just been built on a commanding hill. Charles praised the "grand view" across the Missouri to Council Bluffs. An old photograph I found of the high school shows a surprisingly large and impressive building with a spire rising ostentatiously from the top. It made a strong statement about the civic pride of Victorian Omaha and the importance the town attached to education.

I researched whether the Bucks had ever lived in Brattleboro, but could find no record of them there, so I looked online for Truman Buck in old copies of the *Omaha Daily Bee*. They show that he became a prominent city resident, elected city treasurer in 1882. My wider online search for Buck produced a shocking headline from the *New York Times* of September 22, 1880 (nine years after the Rices' visit).

SILAS M. WAITE ARRESTED. THE ABSCONDING PRESIDENT OF A BRATTLEBORO BANK CAPTURED IN OMAHA. A decided sensation was created in Omaha today by the arrest of Silas M. Waite, the absconding President of the First National Bank of Brattleboro, Vt., whose defalcation amounts to 450 thousand dollars. He was arrested at the house of his brother-in-law, Truman Buck, a well-known and respected citizen . . .

The *Omaha Bee* also reported that Mrs. Buck and Mrs. Waite were sisters, so this led me to discover the link to the Rices and Brattleboro: an 1856 Brattleboro street map shows that Waite and Riley Burdett owned houses two doors apart on North Main Street (now Putney Road). In the 1860s, Charles and Fannie rented an apartment nearby on the same street, so it is likely they knew the Waites as well as the Burdetts, and that Mrs. Waite put them in touch with Mrs. Buck, her sister in Omaha. By the time Waite was arrested in 1880, however, the Rices had left Brattleboro and were living in Worcester, Massachusetts.

Leaving Mr. and Mrs. Buck after dark and looking west over the less-cultivated state of Nebraska, Charles and Fannie had their first glimpse of prairie fires, which "lit up the heavens for miles around, looking like the northern aurora." American Indians called prairie fires the "Red Buffalo." They burned areas of grassland deliberately, because grass regrew quickly and new grass attracted buffalo. When the settlers replaced the Indians, they also replaced the prairie grass, plowing it up to grow crops. When Charles and Fannie visited, settlers had begun the work of cultivating Nebraska, but a lot of the state was still covered in prairie grass, and accidental fires were not uncommon. Imagery of prairie fires can be found throughout contemporary art and literature, with tales of homesteaders and small towns resisting or being overtaken by fire. Artists of the West, such as Frederic Remington and Charles Russell, often used prairie fires to evoke the drama, the beauty, and the terror of frontier life.

Today only 4 percent of the prairie grasslands remain. One place they can be found is the Flint Hills in eastern Kansas, the state bordering Nebraska on the south, where there are eleven thousand acres in the Tallgrass Prairie National Preserve, created in 1996. Burning was reintroduced as part of the preserve's, and nearby ranchers', land management. The modern downside to this practice is that nearby cities complain of air pollution from the smoke. Ranchers now use weather models to help them plan for when burning will have the least impact on air quality downwind.

Charles and Fannie left the flaming spectacle of the prairie fires and went back across the Missouri River to their hotel in Council Bluffs. The next day being Sunday, they attended the local Congregational Church, and heard all about why the congregation was worshipping in the vestry of the unfinished building. A year previously it had been nearly completed when a gale had blown the tower down and badly damaged the building. The pastor went east but raised only half the money needed and resigned. The congregation was awaiting the arrival of a new pastor in a few weeks. Charles wrote, "Some of the western churches struggle for years before they can fairly claim an existence."

The couple attended local churches almost without fail throughout their trip, showing what a big role religion played in their lives. From what I know about Charles' interest in black Americans, I wish he had known about the St. John African Methodist Episcopal Church, which was thriving in North Omaha when they were there. I feel sure he would have jumped at the chance to attend a church established by freed slaves, as he had done elsewhere. (When he and Fannie were on their honeymoon in Virginia in 1866, they had attended a black church in Richmond—and later, when he would spent winters in the South for his health, he would attend a black church in Aiken, South Carolina.)

———

I ARRIVED IN OMAHA at midnight. The train was an hour late. I had arranged to stay for two nights with the Jaynes, members of the Affordable Travel Club that I had joined. I stayed in four such homes on my trip, and I would say that the accommodations were usually better than at any hotel and the people were incredibly friendly and helpful. Moreover, members provide bed and breakfast for a nominal gratuity of fifteen dollars a night. I had told Larry Jaynes that I would cycle to their house, but he insisted on picking me up, saying they lived eight miles from the station. I said that eight miles wasn't far on a bike, but he still insisted, pointing out it would be late, and dark. I was definitely glad that he was there to meet me in his pickup truck. This might have been the beginning of the prairies, but there was no sign of them as we drove along the teeming four-lane Interstate 80 to the Jaynes' house. Once there, I went straight to bed.

Larry and his wife Ruth were both Episcopal priests, although Larry had retired. It was Larry's second retirement. He was previously in the Air Force, where he was the person who made sure no one pressed the nuclear button by mistake. After Larry cooked me a tasty breakfast of an omelet and bacon, Ruth drove me to down-town Omaha in the pickup truck, with my bike still in the back, and dropped me off at the Durham Museum, in the building that was once Omaha's Union Station. Railroad stations with "union" in the name crop up all over the country. Originally every railroad company built its own lines and stations, and in big centers the stations proliferated, so companies finally pooled their money and built union stations to serve several rail lines (eight lines in Omaha).

I stood and admired the 1929 Art Deco building, with its terra-cotta cladding, and then walked around it. It was a monument to the railroad business. Engraved above the north entrances were two quo-tations: "No other improvement . . . can equal in utility the railroad (Abraham Lincoln)" and "Dedicated by the railways of Omaha to the service, comfort and convenience of the people." Carved above the two main entrances were a conductor holding a lantern and a locomotive engineer with his oil can. Over another entrance a civil engineer held a theodolite and a brakeman held a track wrench. I went inside and had to stop again to gaze in admiration at the enormous hall. Its sculp-tured plaster ceiling had gold and silver leaf trim with large bronze, copper, and glass chandeliers hanging high above the black and white terrazzo floor. The original ticket windows, luggage checkroom, large dining room, soda fountain, and barber shop had been restored, but with new uses, and a local artist, John Lajba, had made six life-sized bronze sculptures depicting people who used the old station.

The Amtrak station, where my train had stopped the previous eve-ning, was on the other side of the tracks, clearly the wrong side. The station is located in a small shoebox-like building, similar to many around the rail network that are nicknamed "Amshacks." When the private passenger railroad companies were going out of business in the 1950s, their stations were closed down, and by the time Amtrak was set up in 1971, most stations had already found new uses, often because civic-minded residents fought to save them from demolition. In Brattleboro, the Union Station became the Brattleboro Museum and Art Center, and Amtrak was relegated to the dingy basement, open only when the two daily trains, south and north, pass through. It's about time that American railroads regain some status. Next to the Amtrak station in Omaha stands the empty Chicago, Burlington and Quincy Railroad Station, never quite as grand as its successor, Union Station, but much grander than Amtrak. Why not restore it, and let Amtrak operate in a more attractive building? (Since my visit the station has become a broadcast and web media facility with the sad Amshack still in use next door.)

The museum had some old railroad cars, but none of the 1870s vintage. A bent and grizzled volunteer was a former railroad man and happy to talk. I mentioned that my great-grandparents had stayed in Ogden House in Council Bluffs. His eyes lit up. "Well, well, my wife and I spent our wedding night in that hotel fifty-seven years ago! I'm afraid it went downhill and got very scruffy. It must have been torn down about thirty years ago." We continued to talk about railroads, and when I said I wasn't too impressed with Amtrak's passenger services, he grimaced and spat out bitterly, "Nothing will improve, because there's no money in it."

These days, several organizations lobby for improving rail transportation in the United States. They have a constant battle with politicians who oppose any government funding for train infrastructure, even though government investment has always underpinned the American transportation network. The transcontinental railroad was financed by government bonds and land grants—of nineteen million acres—and the interstate highway system was built with government funds. Even air transportation faltered until the government financed better air traffic control.

Arriving in Council Bluffs and Omaha, facing each other on opposite banks of the Missouri River, I felt I must be getting close to the historic Wild West I was looking for, so I delved into the nineteenth-century history. In 1871, the towns stood at one of the main gateways to the West, a key point in American westward expansion. At that time, it had been almost one hundred years since America had declared its independence from Britain—years of more land being added steadily to the nation. In 1803 the country nearly doubled in size with the addition of land to the west of the Mississippi River (the Louisiana Purchase, from France). It had become accepted that Americans should establish uninterrupted political authority across the continent. As magazine editor John O'Sullivan said, "Our Manifest Destiny is to overspread the continent allotted by Providence for the free development of our yearly multiplying millions."

Some recent historians have said the concept of manifest destiny was a way of justifying territorial expansion, a form of imperialism. It was, but there was also a firm belief that democracy was the best form of government and was God's plan for mankind, giving the republic and its citizens an obligation to bring the blessing of self-government to as broad an area as possible. The belief that it was God's plan implied that Americans were God's chosen people, superior to the "savages" and others. God's plan also included the idea of progress—constant improvement. It was a religious justification for entrepreneurial development and wealth creation.

The assumption of superiority and the commitment to progress were sincere beliefs held by many, but were incompatible with the indigenous peoples' way of life: the Indians weren't using the land "as God intended." When the United States declared independence in 1776, American Indian tribes were treated as sovereign nations and the government signed treaties with them (although it regularly broke them). As the new nation spread towards the west, many tribes drifted or were pushed westward, too.

The agrarian members of the Five Civilized Tribes, who lived in a huge swath of southeastern America, refused to move. President Jackson, determined to open their extensive lands to white settlement, pushed through the Indian Removal Act in 1830, enabling the tribes' expulsion from their ancestral homelands to federal territory west of the Mississippi River. Forced to walk a thousand miles on what became known as the Trail of Tears, many died on the way to the newly designated Indian Territory. And supporters of white settlement were soon demanding this land, too—Indian Territory was obstructing the gateway to the west.

The eastern boundary of Indian Territory in 1834 was the Missouri River. On the eastern side of the river, a small town called Kanesville was one of the crossing points for settlers, swelled by the multitudes that took part in the 1848 Gold Rush to California. William Brown, one of the gold seekers, decided to stop and instead run a ferry from Kanesville (renamed Council Bluffs in 1852) across the Missouri. Settlers weren't legally allowed to establish farms in Indian Territory, so travelers made their way through this land on a trail next to the Platte River, a tributary of the Missouri, and then out of Indian Territory to Utah, Oregon, and California.

Twenty years of federal lobbying and debating led to the Kansas-Nebraska Act of 1854, which formally abolished Indian Territory, apart from what became Oklahoma, and opened up the renamed Nebraska Territory for white settlement. The romantic vision we have of the pioneers and the "Little House on the Prairie" ignores the reality of how they came to be there. The land ceded by the American Indians and available for settlement was federally owned. The ways in which the land was sold and distributed were marked by both high principles and lowdown cunning. The Homestead Act of 1862 made free grants of 160 acres of federal land to settlers, who would get the deeds to the land after they had farmed it for five years.

A system of checks and regulations was missing, allowing unscrupulous entrepreneurs to abuse the process—for example, by carving out a homestead that contained a vital resource, such as water, and then refusing to let adjoining homesteads use it. The railroads also sold some of their land for profit. Town promoters and land speculators got to newly available land as early as possible, hoping to gain an advantage over anyone else thinking along the same lines.

As soon as it looked like Nebraska would be opened up, ferry operator William Brown convinced other local men to invest in a new Council Bluffs and Nebraska Ferry Company. The company was a useful cover for their primary interest, which was surreptitiously surveying the riverside land in Indian Territory. On June 21, 1854, when they had confirmed that the Indians' rights were extinguished, they marked out 350 city blocks on the ground. It would take time to get approval from the infant territorial legislature to incorporate the City of Omaha, so they set up the Omaha Claims Club to protect their claims from anyone else. Club members built shacks on wheels, which they could move about to make it appear that they were living on their claims. The Claims Club became the de facto law, running off newcomers and even hanging a couple of horse thieves.

To be fair, most of the new townsfolk weren't in it just to make money, but to make a new life. They built houses, grew food, and set up basic businesses. Omaha grew quickly at first, but then went through banking failures and a recession, which lasted until the end of the 1850s. In the 1860s, the economy picked up when silver was discovered in Colorado and more people passed through on their way west. Omaha was also successful in an unholy political fight to become the eastern terminus of the railroad to California. The arrival of the Union Pacific Railroad business significantly helped growth. By the time Charles and Fannie arrived, Omaha had a smelter, a hog meat packer, an iron foundry, a carriage works, wholesale houses, grain elevators and mills, gas lamps, a horse-drawn tram line, a hospital, schools, a library, and a fire company. The population had grown to sixteen thousand.

By 1871, Omaha may have left its frontier days behind, but its respectable city institutions and businesses still accommodated a scrappy infrastructure and a lawless underbelly. When Mr. and Mrs. Buck took their guests out to the imposing new high school, no doubt they avoided the less savory saloons and brothels—and a notorious gang of confidence men who targeted visitors and transients. Poker and other card game gambling halls ran day and night. Vote-buying, bribery, and "blind licensing" (the payment in court of "volunteer fines" on a regular weekly basis) were common practices. It wasn't until 1876 that worried citizens united in action to drive out this gang.

Charles acknowledged the elaborate public school building the Bucks showed them, but he also noted serious problems, firmly underlined in his diary. "The hotels are perfectly *horrible*. The sidewalks are *man traps*. The streets *mud holes or sand banks*. Every other building was a Dram Shop. A poem gives a correct description of the place."

*Hast ever been in Omaha,*
*Where rolls the dark Missouri down,*
*And four strong horses scarce can draw*
*An empty wagon through the town?*
*Where taverns have an anxious guest*
*For every corner, shelf and crack;*

*With half the people going west,*
*And all the others going back?*
*If not, take heed to what I say:*
*You'll find it just as I have found it;*
*And if it lies upon your way,*
*For God's sake, reader, go around it!*

(Excerpts from longer poem in *Harper's Magazine*, September 1869)

Omaha in 1871 fit my perceptions of what the gateway to the West would be like, but why didn't Charles and Fannie mention cowboys or the cattle business? The long cattle drives from Texas had started bringing beef north to market several years earlier. Where was this happening in relation to my great-grandparents?

Omaha, I discovered, was the gateway for migration from the East, but not for Texas cattle from the South. The renowned stockyards of Omaha grew up later. When the Rices were there, the important but surprisingly short era of cattle drives was just unfolding two hundred miles south in Abilene, Kansas. People had raised cattle in many places from time immemorial, but throughout the West, in this era, the cattle business was undergoing a major transformation.

My childhood interest in cowboys made me curious to find out more about how it had all come about. I had known for a long time that those cowboy stories were a mixture of fact and fiction, but I wanted to know what the facts were and what the fiction was.

The cattle industry in this part of the world started much earlier, in Mexico. At the end of the sixteenth century, longhorn cattle from the dry grasslands of Spain's Andalucía were brought to Mexico by the Spaniards, to make sure the conquistadores had enough meat to eat. The raising of cattle and other livestock became part of the economy. By the early nineteenth century, cattle were grazing on the arid grasslands of extensive rancheros and Catholic missions in the far northeast of Mexico and were driven long distances to market, even as far as Mexico City. Managing the number of cattle and the distances was achieved by using horses and developing specialist techniques and equipment. The area was far from the political heart of Mexico, sparsely populated, and under attack by hostile Apaches. Not far away, across the border with the United States, American settlers were increasing in number and eyeing the land enviously.

In 1821, Mexicans gained their independence from Spain. They kept the Spanish tradition of letting foreigners, with conditions, come to settle their "empty" lands. In exchange for becoming Mexican citizens and raising livestock, Americans were offered large, cheap, land grants of 4,600 acres, far larger than homesteads being offered by the American government. The climate and the extensive open grasslands made cattle-raising relatively cheap and easy. The American arrivals learned the skills of the Mexican *vaqueros*, and adopted their vocabulary and practical clothing for handling cows on horseback. They quickly outnumbered the native Mexicans and brazenly declared the independent Republic of Texas in 1836.

Nine years later, a one-sided war between the United States and Mexico ended with an American victory in 1848 that caused Mexico to lose one third of its territory and that added Texas and what would become the states of New Mexico, Arizona, California, Nevada, and Utah, and part of Colorado, to the United States. When California livestock-raisers were unable to meet the sudden increase in demand for meat during the California Gold Rush in 1849, Texans began driving cattle to American-held California, and the cattle business in Texas continued to grow and thrive in the 1850s. During the Civil War, between 1861 and 1865, many Texas men joined the Confederate army, and the cattle that were left untended actually multiplied in the ideal conditions of the arid grasslands.

After the war, it was obvious that Texas was a prime source of beef for the potential market in cities further east, and new railroads were coming nearer. In 1867, Joseph G. McCoy, a livestock shipper from Illinois, set up a cattle market in Abilene, Kansas, the nearest point north of Texas that was connected to Chicago via the Kansas Pacific Railroad. McCoy also sent someone south into Texas to look for drovers. (The word cowboy wasn't yet being used.) Cattle drives from Texas to Abilene's market began that year, taking a whole summer to travel a thousand miles on a track that became known as the Chisholm Trail. The cattle were sent by train from Abilene to the

Chicago stockyards, where Philip Armour, Gustavus Swift, and Nelson Morris began building their meatpacking empires.

While the cattle industry was developing in the West, the new industry of mass media was growing rapidly in the East. Better education was enabling more people to learn how to read. Rail transport made rapid distribution across large areas feasible. Dime novels with tales of violence and heroism set in the West were being published in large numbers and were incredibly popular. Countless stories about the frontier were created, often based on real people, but the facts were exaggerated out of all proportion. These in turn influenced the books I read and the television I watched many decades later. I began to understand why the real West in Charles' and Fannie's diaries bore so little resemblance to the West I had imagined they traveled through.

One of the best-known heroes of legend was Wild Bill Hickok. He was never a cowboy, but he was the marshal of Abilene, responsible for keeping order when the rowdy Texan cattle drovers came through in 1871—just as Charles and Fannie passed through Omaha, two hundred miles north. He had been a scout in the Civil War and was already known from an article in the *Harper's New Monthly Magazine* titled "Scout of the Plains Who Had Killed Over 100 Men" (1867). (Evidence indicates he actually killed seven men.) He was an example of the popular press finding real-life figures and turning them into creatures of fantasy. Journalistic exaggerations were claimed as truths and wish fulfillment made these individuals legends, even within their lifetimes. My 1954 copy of the *Pictorial History of the Wild West* had a long chapter devoted to Hickok that scaled down the nineteenth-century exaggerations but still depicted him as a legend. Reading it now, I can detect a tongue-in-cheek flavor to the stories, but I didn't notice it when I was ten.

I would find out more about myth-making when I researched the history of Wyoming, but in Omaha, I left the marvelous museum in the old railroad station to explore more of the city's history on my bike. Larry and Ruth had told me the Old Market was worth visiting. It has been restored to its early-twentieth-century appearance, with old brick warehouses, rough brick-paved streets, and quaint storefronts along covered sidewalks. I peeked into the Soul Desires bookstore that Ruth had recommended, a wee bit suspicious that the books might be too religious. A big black dog, curled up and sound asleep by the window, seemed to offer a homey welcome and I ventured further in, discovering a wide range of books from numerous religious traditions, including one that spoke to "those who don't believe in God but are looking for meaning." I spent a long time reading excerpts and noted down some titles.

The Old Market was lively and attractive but only covered a few blocks. Otherwise, Omaha was ultramodern, with a few old buildings scattered here and there. The nearby Jobbers Canyon, an area of early fruit and vegetable wholesalers, meatpackers, and all sorts of supply people at the hub of late-nineteenth-century Omaha, was designated a national historic district in 1987, but this is an honorary status with minimal legal protection. In 1989, despite a legal challenge by People for Responsible Omaha Urban Development (PROUD), the agricultural industry giant ConAgra demolished the buildings, and its headquarters now cover the site.

To cycle back to the Jaynes' house while avoiding the highway, I worked out a quiet route through residential areas. I enjoy working out cycle routes, a practice honed by years of commuting on a bicycle. The trick is to find ways through that cars can't use. When I look down from a bridge onto a gridlocked road, I smile smugly, knowing I'm likely to arrive just as quickly as those who are driving.

The next morning I returned to the Old Market for a leisurely coffee and decided to look for the Missouri River, the longest river in North America, thinking it would be one thing that would be the same as when Charles and Fannie visited. From the Old Market I cycled past the nondescript ConAgra site and into the Heartland of America Park—pleasant enough and good for cycling, but the river was hidden along this stretch, and inaccessible. After I passed under the intimidating bridge carrying Interstate 480, Route 6, and the Gerald Ford Freeway, I was finally able to approach the riverside, still well-guarded with railings but with the fast-moving water visible to me.

I was at the site where the Lewis and Clark Expedition landed in 1804—where, I discovered, the river had been modernized after all. Back then the river was much wider and shallower. All American schoolchildren know about Meriwether Lewis and William Clark, who explored and mapped the newly acquired Louisiana Territory, on through Oregon to the Pacific Ocean. I loved the story of Sacajawea, the Shoshone woman who translated for their party. When I came on a road trip to the West in 1965 with a college friend, we followed their trail further north.

I could see no sign of the ferry crossing of the 1870s that the Rices used, but I could see the railroad bridge a bit further south, finished the year after their trip. To the north I spotted the new Bob Kerrey Pedestrian Bridge, also for cyclists, arching elegantly across the river. Larry Jaynes had mentioned this new bridge because I'm a cyclist, saying some politicians accused it of being a pork-barrel project that taxpayers shouldn't be funding. I wasn't sympathetic to those accusations—I believe passionately that federal money is appropriate for building infrastructure for nonmotorized traffic, which helps to reduce car use and, in this case, gives cyclists and walkers a way to cross a major river and connect to the network of trails on each side and in two states. Senator Kerrey had obtained a sum of federal money before he left office in 2000, but the city council refused to contribute and the rest of the money was raised privately. Five major bridges connect Omaha and Council Bluffs, and none of them had been open to pedestrians or cyclists. But I was desperately disappointed that I still couldn't cross to Iowa on my bike: the bridge was finished, but not yet open.

I stood and admired it from below. Architecturally, it is surprisingly graceful. Two tall pylons and a delicate tracery of steel cables support the bridge, and the bridge itself curves around from ground level to bridge level and then in an S-shape from the downriver side of the first pylon to the upriver side of the second pylon, curving down to ground level again on the Iowa side of the river. The bridge designers (HNTB, an employee-owned corporation of engineers and architects in Kansas City) noted that a pedestrian bridge gives far more scope for innovation than a car bridge.

Since I was there, the bridge has become a major attraction in its own right, a must-see even for residents and visitors who aren't hikers or cyclists. Its structure is illuminated after dark by an array of LED lights; it has become a venue for outdoor events and has brought the cities of Omaha and Council Bluffs into closer collaboration. Unquestionably it has brought economic benefits to the two cities. It has also strengthened the case being made for building another pedestrian bridge over the built-up area between the newly redeveloped Omaha North Downtown and the Bob Kerrey Bridge, which would give direct access to non-car users. At present, a railroad, and streets parallel to the river, block a direct route for pedestrians and cyclists, who are obliged to travel a much longer distance to cross. I hope it demonstrates a move toward planning for people and not just cars. For too long, European visitors have noticed the extent to which pedestrians aren't catered for in America. Congressional politicians, however, have been cutting federal spending to the bone, putting forward amendments in Congress that would decimate Amtrak and Rails-to-Trails Conservancy (an organization that makes over old railroad corridors for nonmotorized users). Since my trip, I have regularly signed emails to my Vermont congressional representative asking him to oppose this trend.

As I continued cycling north from the Bob Kerrey Bridge, I encountered a large sign next to the road indicating we were coming to the town of Carter Lake. "The people of Iowa welcome you," it announced. Iowa? How could that be? I was in Nebraska, wasn't I? Iowa was on the other side of the wide Missouri River, surely! I made a mental note to find out more, and later unearthed a weird anomaly. A two-square-mile chunk of the state of Iowa actually does sit inside the state of Nebraska. It wasn't there when Charles and Fannie visited. Six years after their visit, a flood cut through the neck of a loop of the meandering Missouri and changed the river's course.

The remnants of the old course, called Saratoga Bend, became an oxbow lake and the town of Carter Lake. Omaha and Council Bluffs started arguing about whose state the area belonged to. In 1890, the Supreme Court decreed that it belonged to Iowa. Although both cities then tried to collect taxes, neither would pay for services or utilities, so the case went back to the Supreme Court. It was finally settled ninety-five years after the event: residents of Carter Lake get their utilities from Nebraska, but go to Iowa schools.

Before I left Omaha, Larry suggested I come with him on a special sightseeing tour. In a leafy residential area with large houses, he pointed to a house on a corner. The house was nothing out of the ordinary. "It's Warren Buffet's house," he said. I knew that Warren Buffet was at that time the richest man in the world. "He brought his family up there and his kids went to local schools. He said they will have to fend for themselves, and not with his millions."

I was impressed by the modesty of the house. Larry approved of Buffet's modest house, too. I had been a bit nervous about staying with people in the conservative Midwest, but Larry and I agreed on almost everything. My visit was during the 2008 election, and we were both crossing our fingers that the United States would elect its first black president. We competed to see who could come up with the worst George W. Bush horror stories. But I did wonder how I would get on with my Mormon host in Salt Lake City.

———

O N AN OCTOBER MORNING in 1871, Charles and Fannie left Omaha to begin the next leg of their train journey, like me, to Salt Lake City in Utah. Not everyone was going by train: Charles noticed many emigrants with wagons heading West, and suggested that residents of Omaha talked as much about going West as the people of New England.

Fannie's account of their departure was terse. "Got up at six and wrote to mother. At eight and a half A.M. we took bus for Omaha, waited for the cars, waited for the ferry and waited for the cars again on the other side of the river." She was probably writing that through gritted teeth. Without a railroad bridge, the transfer for train passengers was by omnibus to the ferry, across the river, and then via another omnibus to the station. It took Charles and Fannie three tedious hours.

Charles grumbled that their luggage was weighed and said to be forty pounds over the limit, so they had to pay an extra three dollars and twenty cents. He added that Fannie was acquiring an attitude about westerners, after having a hard time getting apples and then buying some that were too sour. "Another lie she says, thinks the people out here will lie for money," he wrote. As Charles and Fannie were well-off tourists traveling through, it seems hardly surprising that sellers of food and services were pushing the boundaries. Maybe it was easier for the Rices to complain about service and prices than the discomforts of their upmarket train travel.

# 3

# ACROSS THE GREAT PLAINS
# TO THE ROCKY MOUNTAINS

*October 23, 1871. Mr. and Mrs. Buck met us at the Omaha
Depot to tell us good-bys and God Speed on our journey.*
—Charles' diary

CHARLES AND FANNIE were heading west across Nebraska and then northwest into the Rocky Mountains of Wyoming. I had hoped to follow their route exactly, but about two thirds of the way across Nebraska my train would turn southwest to Denver instead of going across Wyoming. I had particularly wanted to see Wyoming from the train—it is cowboy country, and I drove through it with my college friend and loved it.

I arrived at the dingy Omaha Amtrak station at 9:45 P.M., forty-five minutes early, to make sure I could check in my bike—and discovered the train was more than an hour late. I should have known! I resolved to check lateness before I left for the station in Salt Lake City. I was also charged five dollars to check the bike for the first time.

Eventually setting off, and with nothing to see outside in the dark, I thought about what Fannie and Charles might have been like as people. I read all their diaries, twenty years' worth for each of them. The best ones are their earliest, which reveal more personality than the more hurried adult entries. Fannie's earliest was from 1859, when she was fourteen. She sounded like a typical teenager, busy with school and outings and sleepovers with friends. When I was her age, I was on the phone with girlfriends for hours. In those pre-phone days, they met up face to face. Almost every day Fannie listed five or six girlfriends she had seen, often going "down street" with them to the center of Brattleboro. She made some entries that suggested she had a

*I opened Fannie's compact diary and found a lock of hair,
probably belonging to the daughter of Fannie's close friend.*

crush on someone, but she was coy about his identity, just referring to
"him." (I suspect he was a teacher.)

She had a habit of referring to an incident with emotion but not
explaining what it was about, such as, "This morning something happened but I shan't say what it was." Even in a much later entry, in
June 1871—not long before she and Charles traveled west—she said,
"Charlie told me a very sad thing." Perhaps she had a presentiment
that someone would read her diary some day, and decided always to
be discreet!

Regarding discretion, I discovered that Fannie also kept what she
called "journals." When she was twenty-four, she wrote, "Burned my
old journal, wonder if I ever shall regret it." Reading this reminded
me of my own experience of keeping a diary. I started in 1955, at the
age of eleven, and kept one right through my teenage years. I think
I stopped when I lost my virginity—recording my crushes was one
thing, recording sex was another. As an adult, I have been inconsis-
tent, keeping journals on some holiday trips as a record of what happened and from time to time jotting down my personal thoughts in

a separate place. In my mid-twenties, I found all my teenage diaries in my closet in our family home. I browsed in a few and decided they were silly and juvenile, throwing out all but the earliest ones. I have since regretted that.

The earliest diary I have for Charles is from 1862, a few weeks after he was released from being a wounded prisoner of war. He was twenty-three. Not surprisingly, he recorded some low periods. "I have had the blues for three days and how much longer they will last is more than I can tell. I feel discontented, miserable and almost discouraged." A few weeks later he wrote, "I think sometimes that I would give anything if I could appear like other young men, especially when I am out in their company. It seems to be natural for me to withdraw myself within myself like a turtle."

He recuperated at the Crosbys in Brattleboro for five months and then had to return to army service in Maryland, to a parole camp where soldiers who had been captured and released stayed out of combat until they were matched with an enemy soldier, so both could return to combat. The site of the encampment is now called Parole, Maryland. Once he had settled in, he no longer sounded shy and retiring. On the contrary, he appeared to be in a confident, rather cocky frame of mind. "Started from camp at five o'clock this morning. Obtained some fine apples. Got back to camp just as the men were getting up. Everyone were wanting apples. I told them they could find plenty of them where mine came from." Then later: "Visited the tree under which it is said Gen. Washington planned the battle of Yorktown. Lieut. Col. Kellogg came into camp. He looked as though he was intimately acquainted with whiskey. I also visited the State House. Had a fine view of the bay and surrounding country by the aid of a spyglass. Went to the street this afternoon on a pass forged by myself."

Their diaries barely recorded the couple's courtship. No letters survive, which is a shame. In 1865, when Fannie's father sent Charles to Illinois to work in a grain mill, Charles was obviously homesick. One day he wrote just one sentence: "Received letter from Fannie in the evening, which was better than food." Some other entries in both diaries were too obscure for the meanings to be deciphered. They must have found it difficult to be open about their feelings.

My great-grandparents and I were starting the longest stretch of our train journey, nearly one thousand miles. My journey of twenty-eight hours felt long, but it was half the length of theirs. Before my train diverged into Colorado, our routes coincided where the Great Plains gradually become the Rocky Mountains. From Omaha, at about one thousand feet above sea level, the route continues along the Platte River, rising gradually westwards into a semi-arid climate and hillier terrain. In far western Nebraska, where the town of Sidney is at about four thousand feet, the Rices' route left the Platte River and turned slightly northwest, taking a fairly easy way into the Rocky Mountains and Wyoming and reaching the railroad's highest point at just over eight thousand feet. It continued across a plateau at about six thousand feet until it descended into Utah.

Although both the Rices and I went through Nebraska along the Platte River, I never saw it because it was dark. Charles and Fannie saw it in the daytime and were amazed—it was a mile wide, twice as wide as the Mississippi, but only eight inches deep. It was October, and Charles said the land was brown for as far as they could see, "level as a floor but it had good soil and would support millions of people." Robert Louis Stevenson, author of *Treasure Island* and *Kidnapped*, traveled from England to California by train eight years later. His description of the empty, flat land was more evocative. "We were at sea—there is no other adequate expression—on the plains of Nebraska.... It was a world almost without a feature; an empty sky, an empty earth; front and back, the line of railway stretched from horizon to horizon, like a cue across a billiard-board; on either hand, the green plain ran till it touched the skirts of heaven."

Charles also noticed the emptiness, but he described it in the manner of an easterner who was used to forests everywhere. "Timber very scarce. Occasionally a small belt of cottonwoods. This wood grows very fast." All the timber for the railroad's ties and bridges was brought from much further east, via Chicago. The following year, Nebraskan J. Sterling Morton would successfully establish Arbor Day, which is still celebrated across the United States and in other countries, urging everyone to plant trees. It is estimated that one million trees were planted in Nebraska on the first Arbor Day in April 1872.

Growing up in rural, wooded New England like Charles and Fannie, I took trees for granted. They regenerate so quickly that one of my family's annual chores was "brush-cutting" of any new saplings in the unmown glades around the house. When the dairy business left Vermont's meadows for cheaper pastures to the west, the woods quickly covered the open meadows unless they were mowed. More recently, I have learned that trees keep carbon dioxide out of the atmosphere, so planting more trees has a contemporary benefit that we should take advantage of. But we live and learn. A prairie ecologist recently urged people not to plant trees in Nebraska's open prairie grasslands because of the negative effect trees have on a prairie habitat, and to confine any tree planting to towns and places with trees already. Prairie habitats are really important, with their own biodiversity that helps keep the planet in balance.

In contrast to author Robert Louis Stevenson's image of empty Nebraska, Crofutt's *Trans-Continental Tourists' Guide* of 1871 described verdant crops of wheat, oats, corn, fruits, and vegetables. It seems incredible, but the author was describing what he must have imagined would be there in the future—it wasn't what passengers looked out on in 1871. It is likely he believed in the then-current saying, "The rain follows the plow." The premise of this theory was that human habitation and agriculture through homesteading effected a permanent change in the climate of arid and semi-arid regions, making these regions more humid. The theory was widely promoted in the 1870s as a justification for the settlement of the Great Plains, a region previously known as the "Great American Desert." Unfortunately, it was based on a few years of temporarily higher rainfall. Many pioneers drawn by the promoters' glowing hype went bust because of droughts, until later farmers learned to dig deep wells and build windmills to pump up the water that they discovered was stored underground in porous rock, sand, and gravel, now called the Ogallala Aquifer.

When I visited Omaha's Durham Museum, there was an informative but alarming exhibit about the Ogallala Aquifer, explaining the huge environmental problems with water in Nebraska. Nebraska's economy is heavily dependent on farming—growing grain crops and raising livestock—and this is only possible because of irrigation, using water from underground. The aquifer lies underneath eight states and is the main water supply for the Great Plains region. It waters more than one quarter of all irrigated acreage in the United States and provides drinking water to four out of every five people living above it. For many years, more water has been extracted than is being replaced. When I got involved in tackling the crisis of climate change, my first concern was about using less energy. I didn't think about water, since Britain tends to be a rainy country. The Ogallala Aquifer exhibit opened my eyes to the problems of water in dryer climates.

Since I saw that exhibit, the region has experienced terrible droughts and the aquifer is in even more serious trouble. It is essential that the rate of water use be significantly reduced, but many years of trying have had poor results. Will new initiatives address the problem adequately? I have also discovered that climate change has damaging effects on wetter climates, like that of Britain. Since I returned from this trip in 2008, heavy rainfall and serious flooding have been happening more frequently.

Climate change, reducing fossil fuels, growing trees (or not), water—I was adding to my knowledge about these issues on this trip. None of them were relevant to Charles and Fannie. They had different issues. At a station a couple of hours after leaving Omaha, Charles wrote something I found shocking. "We saw our first Indian, one of the 'bloody scalpers' of the Pawnee tribe, not a bold self-reliant brave, but a sneaking savage, ashamed to stand forth and show himself." Charles' sneering comment prompted me to find out what was behind his response.

I started by finding out about the Pawnee and their contact with whites. They had arrived in the Great Plains around 1600, settling along the Loup, North Platte, and Republican Rivers in present-day Nebraska and Kansas. They became a powerful tribe with four distinct bands, keeping large herds of horses, many obtained by raiding other tribes to the south. In 1800, they were still combining hunting, farming, and gathering in a successful adaptation to their environment.

The biggest threat to American Indians from white contact was the European diseases that they had no immunity to. When Charles saw the Pawnee, his tribe had been decimated by these diseases.

The population before 1800 has been estimated at ten to twenty thousand, but by 1870, it was only two and a half thousand. Because of differing lifestyles, some tribes were more affected than others. Agricultural/nomadic tribes who farmed as well as hunted, such as the Pawnee, spent much of their time in villages, so diseases spread to more people. Nomadic tribes who only hunted, such as the Sioux, kept moving about in smaller groups, so diseases were localized and fewer people were affected. Nomadic tribes consequently gained relatively more power. The Sioux to the north had also profited by trading American buffalo furs with French traders, so they were in the ascendancy and expanding their power at the expense of Nebraska tribes.

The Pawnee were reduced by half in a smallpox epidemic in 1801, but managed to recover. In the 1830s they were hit again by smallpox, influenza, and whooping cough. This time, the Sioux were breathing down their necks and took advantage, frequently raiding their villages, killing them, stealing horses, and starting prairie fires to drive off buffalo and other game the Pawnee wanted to hunt. They seriously impeded the Pawnee ability to grow their corn, beans, and squash and to hunt enough buffalo. Meanwhile, the Pawnee were also under pressure from the increasing numbers of emigrants tramping through their Platte River land on the Emigrant Trail, shooting game, fishing, cutting down trees for firewood, and depleting other resources the Pawnee depended on.

Because they were starving and desperate, the Pawnee began to sign treaties with the American government, ceding their land in exchange for annuities and promises of protection. In 1833, they gave up thirteen million acres south of the Platte, to be used in part to relocate the Delaware tribe that was made to leave Ohio. The annuity money worked out to be just over one cent an acre. Their bad luck continued, with more disease, famine, and attacks. In 1848, they gave up land for the construction of Fort Kearney. After the 1854 Nebraska-Kansas Act that opened up Nebraska for settlement, they signed a treaty, in 1857, to give up their remaining land, apart from 288 thousand acres on the Loup River that was designated a reservation.

On the reservation, the Pawnee found themselves increasingly constrained by the bureaucracy of the Bureau of Indian Affairs and its agents, who were underfunded, generally ineffective, and sometimes corrupt. The Pawnee needed the income generated by scouting for the army, but having warriors away meant their villages were more vulnerable to the Sioux. They complained to an agent that the position of the newly allocated reservation was even closer to their enemies, but he took no notice. One of the conditions of the treaty was that all the Indians had to move to the designated reservation land. Most bands did, but not all. When the Sioux unsurprisingly increased their attacks, the Pawnee chiefs asked the agent to let them buy guns for their defense, but the request was refused—because not all the bands had complied with the treaty by moving to the reservation. It was a catch-22. Meanwhile, the opening of the rest of Nebraska for settlement meant the stream of settlers became a flood, and many staked claims around the reservation. Conflict with the settlers over timber, cattle, and horses increased.

On the day before Charles and Fannie saw the Pawnee at Jackson Station, while Mr. and Mrs. Buck were entertaining them in Omaha, local newspapers were reporting the end of a sorry saga for the Pawnee. In March 1869, army troops in Kansas had attacked a party of fourteen Pawnee braves who were going home after being honorably discharged from US military service. Nine of the fourteen Pawnee were killed. The evidence against the soldiers was irrefutable because the Pawnee guns hadn't been fired, but no one was even charged, much less convicted.

Two months later a white man was murdered near Jackson in Nebraska and the Pawnee were suspected. When officials asked the Pawnee chiefs to produce the suspects, one chief asked if the killers of the nine Pawnee were also to be delivered up. Another chief then proposed that the Pawnee would say nothing about "the men we have lost by the whites, if you will say nothing about the white man who has been killed." The official responded by threatening to withhold annuities due the tribe, forcing the chiefs to give in.

The trial in November 1869 was a farce. The defense lawyer was inept, no one interpreted for the Pawnee, and they were all convicted on circumstantial evidence. This verdict was overturned on a jurisdictional issue and the case was then tried again, still in Nebraska, but without the defendants present because of fears they would be lynched on their way to the trial. They were convicted again. The verdict was appealed again, but bureaucratic bungling continued to affect the case. Finally, while Charles and Fannie were in Omaha, the four men were released by a judge who must have decided that justice wasn't possible. It has since emerged that the white man almost certainly was murdered by a Pawnee—but not one of the accused. It is likely that he was killed because the Pawnee believed, with some reason, that he had stolen two horses, but this mitigating circumstance never emerged in the legal process.

Alcohol is often cited as a major factor in destroying the Indian way of life, but Pawnee chiefs, unlike most other tribal leaders, managed to keep this white import away from their tribe's members. It wasn't enough. After a battle in 1873, when 350 Pawnee were attacked and many slaughtered by a Sioux war party of over a thousand, the Pawnee gave up their long struggle to stay in their homeland. In 1875 and 1876 the remaining two thousand Pawnee moved to what was left of Indian Territory in Oklahoma, alongside the Five Civilized Tribes, removed earlier. The Sioux attack might have been the final straw, but the Pawnees' misfortune to live right across the middle of a major gateway to the West was the more important factor.

It didn't take me long to realize that Charles' comment about the "sneaking savage" simply reflected the mainstream thinking of the time. He and Fannie most likely had a copy of George Crofutt's guide, which said, "The white actual settlers in the country venture to rashness, are hospitable to a fault . . . while their word of honor is always worth more than their bond. But Indians—they are lazy, filthy, and too mean for fish-bait." Even Horace Greeley, a prominent reformist New York newspaper editor who was passionate about the abolition of slavery, said of the Indians, "These people must die out—there is no help for them. God has given this earth to those who will subdue and cultivate it, and it is vain to struggle against His righteous decree." Greeley said this in 1858 after traveling through Kansas, which he described as "the very best corn-lands on earth," where he had observed the

Delaware and Potowamie Indians sitting outside their lodges and doing nothing at the height of the planting season. The gulf between the two cultures' approach to land use was unbridgeable.

I found it easier to understand these attitudes as a product of their time when I discovered a journal entry I had made on my 1965 trip west with my college friend. We had driven through northern Montana toward the Glacier National Park when I wrote, "Drove through the Blackfeet Reservation. It's sad that the present Blackfeet live in apathetic poverty on these lands, not wanting to improve their lot. But who wouldn't want to live and let live in such lovely country? If I were a Blackfoot, I would welcome government support and the opportunity to spend afternoons fishing in blue lakes set off against the golden plains and the green cottonwoods. Or just ride my pony for mile upon empty mile." I cringed at my naïve assumptions about the Blackfeet's situation, but in the 1960s they were probably shared by many. Is it possible that just as many Americans today take the view that the Indians were wronged, and that recovery from that wrong is taking a painfully long time?

———

A S THEIR TRAIN crossed Nebraska, Charles and Fannie continued to get glimpses of the Emigrant Trail (also known as the Oregon Trail), the route running next to the River Platte that had been used since the early 1800s by horse and ox-drawn wagons traveling to Oregon and California. It was still in use, but the railroad had begun to provide relatively inexpensive emigrant trains that took most of the traffic. Although they had seen families traveling in wagons in Omaha, Charles referred to the "old Emigrant Road," as if it were already in the past, reminding him of childhood stories of narrow escapes from prairie fires by early settlers. Charles might also have been influenced by reading Crofutt's guidebook, which told of the old days of wagon transport, injecting a nostalgia that helped create the mythic frontier for tourists.

George Crofutt, whose early guidebook was probably the most popular one used by travelers, was influential during the rapid development of the West. He was an educated easterner who had been bankrupted in the Financial Panic of 1857 and who then joined the Gold Rush to Pike's Peak in Colorado. He found no gold, but he became a long-haul freighter carrying supplies to army forts, stage-coach stations, new railroad camps, and emigrants' service "ranches" along the Emigrant Trail.

He believed that transport was the key to progress and saw the proposed railroad not as a threat to his haulage business but as an opportunity to use his experience and knowledge to get back into the more lucrative business of publishing. He was the first to promote the term "trans-continental," which was so good at conveying the connection of the new railroad with the rest of America. He became what Victorians called a booster, selling the West to visitors who might also be potential settlers or investors. It was never enough for him to describe the beauties of the landscape. He also had to describe its potential for development. Indians were despised, because they were an obstacle to progress.

On our longest stretch on the train, both my diary and the Rices' diaries indicate that we were getting used to traveling in our isolated cocoons on wheels. Charles and Fannie had boarded a Pullman Palace sleeping car. Nineteenth-century passenger car designers clearly understood their customers. Illustrations of that era's trains show that they were made to resemble Victorian drawing rooms, with elaborately carved wood, heavy curtains, and fancy plush upholstery. The carriages felt like a home away from home, a slice of Eastern city life, and they created a shared sense of order, comfort, and familiarity in the face of rapid social change.

Victorians believed that the good home imparted Christian values, exerting a civilizing influence. Public domesticity should do the same, they thought: a good antidote to the disruptive effect of things like westward expansion, the spread of the factory system, urban growth, and immigration. The material gains of luxurious furnishings were also looked on as a reflection of hard work and religious faith, considered the bedrock of American progress.

One Englishman traveling in 1873, however, wasn't impressed by the homey decor of his Pullman car. J. W. Boddam-Whetham complained that there weren't any hooks for hanging hats, coats, and other garments, or any place to put boots. "The horrors of that first night in a Pullman car are indelibly impressed on my mind. The atmosphere ran a close heat with that of the Black Hole of Calcutta."

Sand was a constant irritant on trains, flying into the carriages from the roadbed underneath. Susan Coolidge, in her book of practical advice for ladies, wrote:

> I should advise everybody to be provided with two linen dusters. Dust is the great foe to comfort on the Pacific Railroad. No brushing, no shaking removes it. It sifts, it penetrates, it pervades everywhere. After two or three days you grow to hate yourself. Some ladies whom we met wore barège caps, which drew tightly with an elastic cord over all their hair and kept it free from dust. This was an admirable device, and I recommend it." [Barège was a sheer fabric woven of silk or cotton and wool, named after a town in France.]

Between Omaha and Salt Lake City, we were on the train for such a long stretch that we had plenty of time to get to know our fellow passengers. Charles and Fannie made some friends on this journey whom they kept in touch with for the rest of their trip. Charles described the men as traders, merchants, and missionaries, and there were also two women who were teachers from fire-ravaged Chicago, who were going west to start a new life.

My community was the whole train, whereas Charles' and Fannie's was only one carriage, but both were sociable gatherings. I would have a conversation with someone and then bump into them later on and continue the chat. The casual sociability of a long-distance train is a major advantage of this form of travel, perhaps rivaled only by that found on ocean liners in their heyday. At one point, I got to talking with a young woman while we were waiting to be served in the café. She had been hearing about me from an English couple I sat next to in the Observation Lounge, and was eager to say to me: "Traveling on the train across the country with a folding bike—that's really cool! I'd love to do that."

Another time, I found myself standing with a few other passengers in the vestibule at the end of a carriage, and as one does, I asked a middle-aged woman where she was going. "Back home to Denver," she said. So I asked her where she had been. "To a family reunion in New York City." She paused, but then, with a broad smile and shining eyes, went on: "It was a reunion organized by some of my children. I have thirty-four adopted children." I checked that she had really said "thirty-four," and remarked that I didn't think Britons would ever be allowed to adopt that many children. How had she managed it? She explained. "I used to be a foster mother, but I didn't agree with what the foster agency was doing. One child I fostered was returned to his parents and then badly abused. I started adopting instead, so I knew I had the children permanently." I still couldn't believe she had been allowed to adopt so many children, but her story rang true.

Later on, in the Observation Lounge, the woman next to me said she had been born in New Mexico and was a homeopathic doctor still living there. She was attractive, in her fifties, with shoulder-length fair hair. She described her school days in New Mexico. "Everyone else was darker than me because of their Mexican and Indian backgrounds, while I had blonde hair and light skin. I stuck out, so I was teased and bullied." She added, "And yet my own ancestors, not so far back, also included Cherokee and Choctaw Indians, two of the tribes that had been on the Trail of Tears in 1831."

I warmed to her open attitude to cultural diversity. I regard these differences as the human contribution to biodiversity, so I would be delighted to find some Indian blood in my line. It's unlikely, though; I know a lot about my family history, and most of my ancestors came from England in the 1620s to 1640s. None of the men were trappers or traders. I have not found anyone who wasn't an upright member of the community, so I doubt they would have gotten to know any Indians except at a distance.

My uncle Howard, who got me interested in our family history, told me what I think is the most interesting story about our family's contact with Indians. My seven-times-great grandmother Elizabeth Corse was captured by Indians in 1704 in Deerfield, Massachusetts, along with her daughter. Because she was slowing the party down, Elizabeth was killed on the journey to French Canada. Her daughter married a French Canadian and never returned to Deerfield. Then

Uncle Howard added, "But her son James was not captured—and he's your six-times-great grandfather!" I was thrilled with this story.

On the sociable train, I realized that I enjoy meeting people who are different. I think Charles and Fannie preferred the comfort and safety of meeting people similar to themselves, people from the merchant and professional classes. Unlike British trains, the earliest American railroad cars adhered to Americans' supposed classlessness, and all carriages were the same for everyone. Class divisions crept in surreptitiously, however, as different levels of service were introduced, determined by price if not labeled by class. Americans' vaunted egalitarianism didn't rule out a monetary pecking order. Charles and Fannie paid an extra fee for berths in sleeper cars and must have paid more for the commissary car they traveled in from Clinton, Iowa, to Omaha.

I was annoyed to find the pecking order affected me, too. Because I was in a coach car, I found myself at the end of the line for booking a seat in the California Zephyr's dining car, so I didn't get in until 9:45 P.M. First choice went to those in the much more expensive sleeper cars, whose meals were included in the price of their tickets.

The third class in the nineteenth century was the emigrant train, for the aspirant poor trying to better themselves. Robert Louis Stevenson took this train to save money. (He was joining a married woman he was in love with, and his parents refused him funds.) The fare from New York to San Francisco was sixty-five dollars, compared to the one hundred and forty-three dollars paid by Charles and Fannie. The train had three carriages, one for women and children with their menfolk, one for men traveling alone, and one for the Chinese. In practice, Stevenson said, the single men were so numerous that they spilled over into both of the other carriages.

The carriages were plain throughout, with wooden planks as benches on each side of the aisle. Sleeping arrangements involved every other bench being turned around to face the one next to it, whereupon a bed board and cushions were laid down between them, making a couch wide enough for two. This required two passengers to agree together to pay for the bed board and cushions. The passenger next to Stevenson refused to share with him. The lack of facilities meant the emigrant cars smelled. Charles and Fannie never mentioned them, but their train almost certainly included some emigrant cars.

During my night on the train in Nebraska, I outfoxed the passengers in the expensive sleepers, enjoying an excellent sleep lying on a seat in the Observation Lounge. I even had it all to myself. Everyone else disappeared when views of the scenery went down with the sun.

On the rest of the train journey from Omaha to San Francisco, the Rices took their meals at "eating stations," where the train stopped and passengers were given half an hour to buy and eat a meal in a station restaurant. A widely circulated but unsubstantiated story suggested that food was purposely served too hot to be eaten in the limited time, and was re-served to those on the next train. A passenger traveling west in 1869 described one way in which people coped with the short stops at eating-stations. They took a newspaper with them, filled up their plates, and then, when the whistle blew, wrapped the uneaten food in the newspaper and took it back to the train. The only alternative to the rarely available commissary car was a luxurious hotel-car with staff, which had to be booked in advance and added to the train, and which was affordable only for the very wealthy.

While Charles and Fannie slept through western Nebraska, an army scout named William Cody was probably asleep, too, at Fort McPherson, a few miles from the railroad tracks. He would later become better known as Buffalo Bill, the master of ceremonies for a traveling show he started in 1883 called Buffalo Bill's Wild West, whose enormous success and popularity, spanning thirty years, established an enduring vision of the Wild West for people in America and in Europe; on one of the eight European tours, in 1887, Queen Victoria attended a performance. In October 1871, when the Rices' train passed the fort like a ship in the night, Cody was still establishing his reputation as a buffalo hunting guide, having just finished guiding a party of easterners on a hunt in western Nebraska. A couple of months later, he guided a party that included the Grand Duke Alexis of Russia. Meanwhile, as an army scout based at Fort McPherson, he kept track of the Indians and hunted buffalo to supply food to the army and the Kansas Pacific Railroad.

After their night's sleep through western Nebraska, Charles declared that the breakfast he and Fannie ate at Sidney Station, the last town in the state, was satisfactory. Leaving Nebraska meant leaving the lower plains and entering the higher plains and mountains of Wyoming, but it also meant leaving the Union and entering the Wyoming Territory, which wasn't made a state until nearly thirty years later. When I had arrived in Nebraska, I had felt I was approaching the Wild West—but Wyoming was the Wild West without any doubt whatsoever.

Although I was fascinated by the West as a child, I was nineteen before I first went there, in 1963. The United States was still in a post-war boom for celebrated road trips. Nat King Cole sang "Get Your Kicks on Route 66." Jack Kerouac's novel *On the Road* told about members of the Beat Generation driving across the country and searching for meaning via sex and drugs. Ray Charles recorded a hit song that is still one of my all-time favorites, "Hit the Road, Jack." Even as I write, the refrain bounces in around my head: ". . . and don't you come back no more, no more, no more, no more. Hit the road, Jack, and don't you come back no more."

In that year, my family embarked on its own road trip, which felt pretty adventurous for us small-town New Englanders. We drove to the West Coast from Vermont in a station wagon, towing a trailer behind us and using a route, due west, that included a stretch of Canada and a ferry across Lake Michigan. Once we got to the Rocky Mountains in Wyoming, I was entranced by the soaring alpine crags of the Grand Tetons and the unbelievable sheer granite faces of Yosemite Valley in the Sierra Nevada of California. San Francisco was the most beautiful American city I had ever seen. Within three years, I traveled to the West four more times, the highlight being a summer camping tour of the Rocky Mountains with a college friend. I had fallen in love with the place.

# 4

# WYOMING: COWBOY
# AND INDIAN COUNTRY

*October 24, 1871. Breakfast at Sidney. Antelope,*
*prairie dogs and wolves abundant. Rising the mountains*
*gradually. Stopped at Laramie for supper, saw in the*
*distance a herd of buffaloes, saw the first Chinese.*
—Fannie's diary

FANNIE AND CHARLES continued through the Rocky Mountains without seeing any cowboys or Indians. On my diversion through Colorado, I thought nostalgically of my favorite trip to the West. In summer 1965, a college friend, Betty, and I set off for the Rocky Mountains from Boston in my much-loved VW Beetle, intent on exploring the scenes from our childhood history books about cowboys, Indians, and the early American explorers of the West. We crossed the Missouri River in South Dakota into Wyoming, followed the Lewis and Clark Trail north into Montana to the source of the Missouri, and then continued to Glacier National Park in the northwestern corner of the state. We came back through Wyoming to Colorado. Wyoming was remote and barely settled when Charles and Fannie passed through. Even now, it has the second lowest density of population per square mile in the United States, and Montana has the third lowest. (Alaska has the lowest.)

When Lewis and Clark traveled through, in 1804, fur trappers and traders were still active, but for the most part this wilderness was left to the Sioux, the Cheyenne, the Blackfeet, the Crow, the Arapaho, and several other smaller tribes. Their right to the land was confirmed by the Treaty of Fort Laramie in 1851. In 1862, however, gold was discovered along the banks of Grasshopper Creek in southwest Montana, then part of the Idaho Territory. Despite the country being torn apart by the Civil War, in less than a year nearly three thousand prospectors went to look for gold (were they also avoiding the possibility of being drafted to fight?). Many used a new trail from Cheyenne, Wyoming, along the same rivers Lewis and Clark had followed. Despite the treaty guaranteeing this land to the American Indian tribes, the federal government supported the Bozeman Trail that now cut through it; gold was needed to finance the war effort, and the three forts established along the trail would be useful for protecting the route of the transcontinental railroad, to be built through the Wyoming Territory to the south.

The Indians regarded the trail as a major threat to their way of life and were determined to stop it. For the first time since the Indians had grudgingly given way to the invaders, the Sioux, led by Red Cloud, formed a large and aggressive confederacy with the Cheyenne and Arapaho, then put up a concerted effort to drive the invaders out. Red Cloud knew that direct confrontations with the whites' superior weapons were hopeless, so he adopted what we now call guerrilla warfare. The Indians' frequent attacks on the forts and harassment of wagon trains were so successful that the American government was forced to sue for peace. The Fort Laramie Treaty of 1868 again guaranteed the tribes ownership, in perpetuity, of land and hunting rights in South Dakota, Wyoming, and Montana. The Powder River Country was henceforth to be closed to all whites. Chief Red Cloud is remembered as one of the few Indians in American history to make the federal government back down from achieving an important territorial goal.

So when Charles and Fannie crossed the southern part of Wyoming in 1871, the Bozeman Trail was no longer used and the Indians had been pacified by the new treaty. Charles' withering comment about the Pawnee at the Nebraska train station said it all. Indians were no longer important and travelers could enjoy more prosaic sights, like prairie dogs. Charles wrote a long description of their amusing behavior, noting that they stood up on their hind legs to watch the world and chatter to each other, but vanished into their burrows when disturbed. (These days, prairie dogs have a more controversial status: some view them as pests to be exterminated, others as endangered species that need protecting. I hope the outcome is protection, but I also hope it addresses the problems they present.)

Charles and Fannie could not have known that the peace with the Indians was a temporary interlude. Two years after their trip, gold was found in the Black Hills to the north, in the land that that had been granted to the Indians "in perpetuity" five years earlier. Half-hearted attempts were made to enforce the treaty, but the flow of prospectors and settlers carried on. The Indians were asked to give up the land, but they refused. In 1876, while Charles and Fannie were celebrating the first centennial of the American Declaration of Independence in Brattleboro, the army was ordered to launch a campaign to force the Sioux, Cheyenne, and Arapaho tribes to return to their reservations. In June 1876, Lt. Col. George Armstrong Custer and his Seventh Cavalry Regiment joined the campaign. Many books have been written about the Battle of the Little Bighorn, but the final outcome was straightforward. Custer and his company were all killed in the most well-known Indian victory in the history of the West, which came to be known as Custer's Last Stand.

Betty and I drove north on Lewis and Clark's route along the Little Bighorn River, stopping at the famous battlefield that in the 1960s was mostly a bare hill, without the later walkways, interpretation signs, and other tourist paraphernalia. A small sign about the battle mentioned that it happened in 1876, and I realized with surprise that it was five years after my great-grandparents' trip. From that moment, the threat of Indian attacks hung over my mental image of the traveling couple, an image I would have to revise when I eventually learned more about the history.

In the wake of Custer's defeat at the Little Bighorn, the army altered its tactics, playing the friendly tribes off against the hostile ones and sending another commission to negotiate. Congress passed a law extinguishing all Sioux rights outside the Great Sioux Reservation, although the Sioux never legally ceded their land. Although George Crofutt had described the Indians as "lazy, filthy, and too mean for fish-bait," even he could see the justice of their cause in this case. In his 1878 guidebook, he wrote, "We are no 'Indian Lover' but if the Government had the right to build these posts, they should never have abandoned them; having abandoned them and treated with the Indian as an equal, where is our boasted 'civilization,' when though the lands do contain gold, we take them without a 'thank you' as the elephant would crush a toad. Does might make right?"

The Sioux never accepted the breaking of the treaty and have been fighting in the courts for the return of their land since 1921. Opponents have argued that the Sioux acquired that land by pushing out other Indians, but the Sioux said that they had lived there a long time and that many parts of the land were sacred to them. They particularly resent one of the relatively recent changes to the land, the faces of four presidents carved into a sacred mountain. I visited Mount Rushmore in 1963 on our family trip. I don't recall anyone mentioning the Sioux, but I don't think their claim came to prominence until the American Indian Movement occupied the site on the Fourth of July, 1971, after Indians began campaigning for their civil rights. They said it was sacred, carried out a cleansing ceremony, and declared Mount Rushmore a Shrine to Hypocrisy instead of the Shrine of Democracy.

In 1980, the US Supreme Court accepted that the seizure of the land in 1877 was illegal, but the offered remedy of monetary compensation instead of the return of the land is still being debated amongst the Sioux; $106 million plus interest is being held for them in the meantime. In 2004, the first park superintendent of Indian ancestry, Gerard Baker, opened up a dialogue with local Indian groups, resulting in the establishment of Heritage Village, a cluster of Sioux tepees and Sioux talking about their culture.

In 2010, President Obama asked James Anaya, the UN Special Rapporteur on the rights of indigenous peoples, to carry out an investigation. In relation to the unsettled dispute about the Black Hills, Anaya said, "Some kind of restoration, should occur . . . by which the Lakota people could have a greater access to the Black Hills, be more present there, and that place represent again a part of the people, the Lakota people, as opposed to simply representing their defeat and the negative side of history." (The Sioux are also known as the Dakota or the Lakota, depending on their dialect.) And Mount Rushmore, visited by nearly three million people a year, remains an iconic, some would say ironic, tribute to the lofty ideals of American democracy.

The Americans' original policy of pushing the Indians westward changed in the mid-nineteenth century to confining them to reservations. After the Civil War ended in 1865, it changed even more severely to making them assimilate, culminating in the policy of terminating tribes altogether, beginning in the 1940s. I was shocked to discover that President Kennedy, my generation's Camelot hero, signed an order in 1962 to terminate the Ponca tribe, which lived near Omaha in Nebraska. (After years of campaigning, the Ponca Restoration Bill was signed into law in 1990.)

In 1944, the Indians formed the National Congress of American Indians (NCAI), the first major intertribal association, and began to campaign against the threat to their identity posed by the new policy. "Self-determination rather than termination!" was the NCAI slogan. President Kennedy may not have heard them, but Indian voices were getting louder, and in 1968 President Johnson finally declared his support for Indians' right to self-determination. Protests continued, but finally the right to tribal sovereignty was reestablished by law.

In her groundbreaking book of 1940, *A History of the Indians of the United States*, Angie Debo had described the Indians' outlook simply and clearly: "The Indian wanted to be with his own people, to preserve his inner values, his cultural integrity. To this desire he owes his remarkable record of survival, the preservation of his distinctive identity, through centuries of encroachment by a more numerous and aggressive race." Debo, a Western woman who rose up through the ranks of academia in lesser-known universities, was ignored in her day—either because she was a woman or because she was way ahead of her time.

The recognition of tribal sovereignty in the 1970s exempted Indian reservations from state jurisdiction, including taxation, and many tribes turned to providing gambling (more often called gaming) in states that prohibit it. Gambling is controversial and many people frown on it, including many Indians, but it has raised much-needed money. There is little demand for gaming in the sparsely populated states of South Dakota, North Dakota, and Nebraska, so the Sioux have begun tapping a different money-making resource: wind. Seven tribes comprising the Great Sioux Nation are developing wind resources in their tribal areas by setting up the public Oceti Sakowin Power Authority. A spokesperson said, "We are honored to have this opportunity to pursue our sacred trust as responsible stewards of the earth, not only on the Mother Land of our tribes, but also as members of the global community." In this way they are continuing their tradition of working with nature, not against it. I knew little about American Indians' culture and beliefs, so it was heartwarming to discern that the Indians' traditional relationship with the environment was a sustainable one that assumed that humans are part of nature, rather than separate beings who are trying to tame or conquer it. I resolved to learn more about their approach to living.

At the same time, I found an example of our white culture's opposite take on the environment, north of the transcontinental railroad. The vast Powder River Basin of Montana and Wyoming, which was the former Sioux homeland, is still federally owned and is the site of the two largest commercial open-pit coal mines in the world. The Powder River Basin produces 43 percent of the nation's coal and more than 13 percent of all United States carbon dioxide emissions.

Coal is the dirtiest fossil fuel, so it is first on anyone's list of fossil fuels to be phased out and replaced by alternative energy sources. Scientific evidence shows clearly that if we don't keep most of the remaining fossil fuels buried and unburnt, we face climate chaos and economic disaster. Coal mining in the Powder River Basin area is also destroying wildlife habitats and polluting the air and water. Several environmental groups, with Indians among them, are campaigning against coal being mined in Wyoming, Montana, and other Western states. They are also campaigning against mega trucks driving through their communities with equipment for mining the Alberta tar sands in Canada, and against proposed oil pipelines that interfere with their sacred sites.

The Sioux's development of wind power is joined by many other tribal alternative energy projects in the United States—in wind, solar, geothermal, and biomass energy. American Indian land makes up

2% of the US land base, but contains 5% of all US renewable energy sources. It is so appropriate that American Indians are benefiting from the earth's renewable resources in this way—but there's at least one catch. Some Indian tribes are taking wind farms to task, saying that they endanger bald and golden eagles, birds that are sacred to them. This information pulled me up short and put the Indian culture and beliefs in perspective; conflicts about priorities arise in any culture.

---

BACK IN 1871, the train stopped for passengers to eat in Cheyenne, the first and only town of any size on the railroad through Wyoming. Charles and Fannie decided to forgo the meal and go for a stroll. Charles wrote that land of any value in the area was held by speculators hoping to get "fabulous prices." He noted that the town had a bad reputation for thieves and desperate characters, but a local "vigilance of its best citizens hung several of the thieves and order was restored." Fort D. A. Russell was about three miles north of the station and connected with Cheyenne by a side track. Charles mentioned that officers and their wives often came to watch trains pass because it was welcome excitement in such a remote place. Fort Russell is now the Francis E. Warren Air Force Base, home to intercontinental ballistic missiles.

Cheyenne was smaller and younger than Omaha, but it was also trying hard to become respectable. Its bad reputation was a holdover from a few years earlier when it was an end-of-the-line railroad town. Then, it had the Big Tent, a notorious canvas tent set up in towns as the end of the tracks moved across the country. Inside, customers who spent enough money could get a drink, play a game of cards, dance with a girl, hire a prostitute, and get treated for venereal disease all in one visit. Such mobile tents, along with the lawlessness they attracted, gave these towns the nickname Hell on Wheels—but when the track was finished, the workers and the tents rolled on. Still, the reputation lingered.

Charles and Fannie were only in Cheyenne briefly, so perhaps it isn't surprising that they didn't notice another facet of the growing town. The burgeoning cattle business may still have been two hundred miles south of Omaha, but it had already reached Cheyenne, directly from Texas. Many years previously, John Wesley Iliff, the son of a wealthy Ohio cattle farmer, had left home to seek his fortune. After two years selling provisions to silver miners in Denver, Colorado, he bought some Texas cattle cheaply that were being driven along the Goodnight-Loving Trail. He fattened them up, sold them at a good profit, and then set up another ranch further north, near Cheyenne, where he started supplying beef to feed the Union Pacific Railroad workers. Just seven years after buying his first cattle, Iliff owned nearly twenty-five thousand head of livestock and roughly eight thousand acres of land. He moved his headquarters to Cheyenne, winning contracts to supply army forts and Indian reservations, as well as sending some cattle back east to stockyards in Chicago.

Charles and Fannie wouldn't have mentioned cowboys because the word wasn't yet in common usage, but I am puzzled that Charles, in particular, never mentioned cattle or livestock. When he was staying in San Francisco, he received copies of a paper edited by a Brattleboro friend, F. B Cobleigh, the *Vermont Record and Farmer*, and it always included reports about the weekly markets for livestock. I also found an article in Brattleboro's *Vermont Phoenix* on July 14, 1871, two months before the Rices' departure. Its headline was "Cattle Princes of Texas," and it described in detail how Texans were establishing successful cattle ranches with herds totaling 3.8 million head, the cattle being driven to markets in the southern states, to the north, and to the west. So news of the cattle business had reached the East. I assume Charles hadn't read that article or, if he had, he had dismissed its relevance because it was mostly about Texas, not the part of the West they were going to visit.

Crofutt's guide also promoted the livestock business, using his personal experience of stock grazing during his years as a freighter. He wrote, "It's the best grass country in the world. Stock thrive in this section all the season, without care, excepting what is necessary to prevent them from straying beyond reach." The "section" he mentioned was in Wyoming and Montana Territories: a huge tract of open rangeland that was two hundred by seven hundred miles, federally owned, and unfenced, so it had free grazing, grass, and water year-round.

"The cost of keeping stock in this country is just what it will cost to employ herders—no more."

He also pointed out that there was a market for beef in the West, not just the East. The infrastructure for settlers, towns, and businesses was growing. The army needed supplying. The Indian Agency was shipping beef to Indian reservations as payment in kind (of annuities), because the Indians' traditional source of meat, buffalo, was dwindling. I suspect that, despite the growing evidence of ranching as a development in the West, Charles and Fannie hadn't let go of the long-standing assumption of easterners that westward expansion meant individual yeoman farmers growing a range of crops and keeping some animals.

As Crofutt had pointed out, however, the cattle business was being recognized as a good way to make money with low capital investment. Within a few years, tales of dependable profits of forty percent annually filled the newspapers and livestock journals. It was the heady era of the open range, an important thread in the frontier story. At the top end, new cattle companies multiplied, financed by eastern investors as well as some from Scotland and England. Meanwhile, many a Tom, Dick, and Harry (and some Marys) noticed the potential rewards of the burgeoning cattle business and started their own herds. The grass of the open range, which was free to the first cattle raiser to come across it, was also free to the second, third, and fourth, but the blades of grass weren't limitless. The first or second cattle raisers saw themselves as hardy pioneers and men of enterprise. They saw the third and fourth arrivals as range pirates stealing their grass.

A few weeks after Charles and Fannie passed through Cheyenne, Iliff and other cattle owners met with the governor of the Wyoming Territory and other territorial politicians to discuss how to consolidate their positions. The Wyoming Stock Growers Association was set up in 1872 and, contrary to the notion of yeoman farming, grew to represent a large concentration of private wealth. The members held cooperative roundups in the spring to gather and brand newborn calves, established a registry of brands, and hired stock detectives to track down cattle thieves.

Others who wanted to cash in on this lucrative business knew the federally owned open range was supposed to be free to anyone, and they resented the Stock Growers Association refusing their participation in the roundups and not allowing them the protection of stock detectives. They disliked the ingenious ways the stock growers found to keep grass on public lands for themselves while denying it to competitors, like securing water rights that, in practice, gave them extensive range rights. The ensuing conflicts led to cattle rustling, fence-cutting, and vigilante range wars, the stuff of both fiction and real life.

Meanwhile, the herders of the cows came to be known as cowboys. "Cowboy" is a curious word, having developed so many varied meanings both as correct English and as slang. It was first used in England in the early eighteenth century when it was adolescents who traditionally herded animals, and it was thus an accurate description (a boy tending cows). By 1849, it was occasionally used in the American West for adult cattle handlers, although "herder" and "cowhand" were more common. It took the next thirty years for "cowboy" gradually to enter general usage.

Through the years, "cowboy" has also been a derogatory slang word. During the American Revolution, it was used by Loyalists to belittle Americans who were supporting the British. These days, it is used in the American Northeast for reckless drivers and in Britain for incompetent tradesmen. As the cattle business developed in the West, a distinction arose between the owners of the cattle and the men they employed. Owners were cattlemen, stock growers, or ranchers. The men they employed came to be called cowboys, but they had no status. Some of these cowboys aspired to rise up the pecking order by buying their own stock, aiming to use the free grass and free water to fatten their cattle for market. A few others obtained stock by rustling. The established ranchers in the stock growers associations assumed the worst, so calling someone a cowboy suggested he was a horse thief, robber, or outlaw. A gang that smuggled cattle, alcohol, and tobacco across the border from Mexico into Tombstone, Arizona, was dubbed the Cowboys. Ten years after the Rices' trip, the Cowboys and Wyatt Earp had their infamous gunfight at the OK Corral.

Meanwhile, the open range was changing rapidly. Barbed wire, invented and patented in 1874, was used to enclose some of it illegally.

Then, in the mid-1880s, the Western cattle bubble burst. The boom had rapidly overstocked the ranges, damaging the grasslands and leaving cattle undernourished at the end of summer grazing. A drought further damaged the grasslands and water holes. Then, severe blizzards during some winters killed nearly half the cattle in the Great Plains. Many weakened cattlemen were driven into bankruptcy. The days of the open range, just twenty years after they started, were already over.

The shortness of the era seems to have induced nostalgia for what was so quickly in the past. Buffalo Bill's Wild West show began touring with its combination of authentic reality and entertaining theatre. Buffalo Bill quickly rehabilitated the reputation of cowboys by including them in his show, demonstrating the skills they had developed in using ropes and horses. Cowboys' horse and cattle-handling skills were also being honed with the rise of rodeos, which started as roundups, then became inter-ranch competitions, and then went on to become some of the most important public entertainments in the West.

The open range and the long cattle drives may have ended, but the cattle business continued. Rich cattlemen bought out bankrupt colleagues and consolidated their positions. The Matador Ranch in Texas is a good example of one that survived the bust. In the early 1870s, Hank Campbell, a modest but canny Texan cattle owner, built up a herd of Texas longhorns and later sold them at a good profit, going into partnership with several bankers in northwestern Texas and finally selling on to Scottish merchants in Dundee. With the low costs of the open range and high beef prices, the ranch continued to expand, and with its large size, it survived the mid-1880s crises. In 1952, Fred C. Koch bought it and formed the Matador Ranch, which is now part of Koch Industries, one of America's largest private companies. The sons of Fred Koch, brothers Charles and David, are well known these days as prominent right-wing libertarians who spend tens of millions of dollars supporting candidates for elective office, and have spent millions more funding climate change denial campaigns. Many American ranches made this transition from being a pastoral herding business to a small money-making cog in a mega-corporation.

It isn't the whole story. Some ranches went on a different journey, managing to remain family businesses and surviving by becoming more sustainable. On my 1965 trip with Betty, we drove from Montana back south through Wyoming, passed through Laramie and over the railroad west of Cheyenne, and continued south to Steamboat Springs, Colorado, where we called at the family cattle ranch of my college classmate Ned Fetcher. Ned's father, John, and his brother had bought land and four old log cabin homesteads in the 1940s and gone into ranching. When we visited, John Fetcher was president of the fledgling Steamboat Springs Ski Area. An engineer by training, he was also active in local water conservation and served on the Colorado Water Conservation Board. Over the next few decades, the success of the ski area brought many people to the area, pushing land prices up. By the 1990s, land prices had risen so much that it had become increasingly difficult for ranches to be passed from one generation to the next, because of the high death duties. As a result, more and more ranches were being sold, with the land being used to build houses.

In 1995, Ned Fetcher's brother, Jay, helped to set up the Colorado Cattlemen's Land Trust. This was the first time a livestock association in the United States had formed such a trust. The trust enables landowners to use conservation easements to protect, in perpetuity, their land and its open space, and also its wildlife habitat, agricultural areas, scenic vistas, and historic properties. It provides financial and tax benefits. So far, the trust and landowners have protected over four hundred thousand acres of productive agricultural land, including the one thousand, three hundred–acre Fetcher Ranch. State livestock associations in Wyoming, California, Kansas, Texas, and Oregon have since set up similar land trusts.

It is good that family ranches can avoid being sold for housing developments, but I discovered that the American love of ranching and beef have an unfortunate downside. Beef requires much more land and water to produce than pork or chicken and results in more climate-warming emissions. Cattle are more inefficient in converting food and water into meat because they are so much bigger, having more bone, skin and other tissues besides meat. When compared to staples like potatoes, wheat, and rice, the impact of beef per calorie is even more extreme. With the world population still increasing and more people in developing countries now eating meat, we won't have enough space to grow food for both animals and humans—so we must eat less meat, starting with beef, and more vegetables.

Like so many others, I have enjoyed many a romantic daydream about the iconic Western scenery, with horses and cattle grazing in the picturesque mountain pastures, but this new knowledge clouded those blue skies for me. I'm trying to reduce my carbon footprint and had assumed it was all about using less fossil fuel when traveling and insulating my house. With this realization I decided I should consider not eating meat. And so I became a vegetarian.

———

CHARLES AND FANNIE'S train carried on from Cheyenne to Sherman, the highest point on their route at just over eight thousand feet. The ascent was gradual, but Charles could tell they were in a mountain range because they began to see craggy peaks in various directions. They looked for Longs Peak and Pikes Peak, already famous from silver mining days, which the guidebook said could be seen to the south, but it was too hazy.

Just before reaching Sherman, they went through the first of many snow sheds, erected in places known to collect wind-blown snow. Beginning the descent, they crossed Dale Creek on a trestle bridge over seven hundred feet long and one hundred and twenty feet above the stream. Charles simply recorded that they crossed "the slender structure" and added, with a touch of bravado, "It stands the strains of the several trains which cross it daily." Other travelers told of their terror in crossing the chasm while the bridge swayed in the wind, and two years later passengers reported seeing the wreck of a freight train below.

The coming winter would turn out to be more severe than most. In February 1872, a Boston businessman named Walter Scott Fitz stayed at the same hotel where my great-grandparents lodged in San Francisco, but there is no record of their paths having crossed. On February 28, he wrote a long letter about coming to San Francisco through Wyoming, three months after Charles and Fannie. The train journey that took Charles and Fannie thirty-six hours took Fitz three weeks.

Fitz described in detail the frustrations of heavy snowdrifts blocking their way. Passengers helped with digging a path for the train, and those in Fitz's car joined together to obtain food, utensils, and crockery, making a serviceable griddle pan out of telegraph wire. They amused themselves by reading, playing cards, and singing sacred and popular music in the evenings. Fitz wrote, "Our mess numbered eight persons . . . a mining engineer, proprietor of mines, clothing dealer living in Salt Lake City, retired brewer, a Real Estate broker from Ogden, a lady and son living in Idaho, and one young man who had been dismissed from the Naval Academy for hazing freshmen."

I found this long letter buried on the website of the Central Pacific Railroad Photographic History Museum, which shows how the shapers of popular culture sometimes ignore colorful but peaceful true stories of the American West from my great-grandparents' time and highlight conflict and violence instead.

When this saga was happening, Charles and Fannie were in San Francisco, where they noted the extreme train delays caused by the snow, but only in relation to not receiving their customary mail. Correspondence with friends and relatives was a priority throughout their six months in California, and they carefully recorded trips to the post office, including letters sent and letters received. If they wondered what was happening to the passengers on the snowbound trains, or even heard about them later from Mr. Fitz, they didn't say, although they did record on February 19 (when Fitz's train finally reached San Francisco) that "the Post Office received over two hundred tonnes of mail." My first thought was to shake my head at their capacity to consider this fact more noteworthy than the passengers' experiences, but then I tried to imagine what it must have been like in those days to be cut off completely from friends and loved ones because the expected mail was delayed.

Their own crossing of the high plateau of Wyoming continued in October without incident, apart from sightings of many herds of antelope and some prairie wolves (coyotes). They stopped for a good meal in Laramie—a town named for an early French Canadian trapper,

Jacques La Ramie, who had disappeared in the mountains about 1810. Laramie's population was fewer than nine hundred, but it already had a claim to fame that Charles described in some detail. The first legislature of the Wyoming Territory had passed a bill granting equal political rights to women, probably at the behest of Julia Bright, one of the legislators' wives and a committed suffragette. In 1870, five Laramie residents became the first women in the world to serve on a jury. Charles wrote that at first they were reluctant but finally consented, to universal satisfaction as they "cleared the town of a class whose presence was a moral blight." The United States as a whole didn't approve universal women's suffrage until 1920. Cattle King John Iliff was persuaded in 1873 to move from Cheyenne back to Denver by his wife— who didn't like the idea of sitting on a jury because she would have to "mingle with her social inferiors"!

Women in the early frontier narratives tended to be stereotyped as the tough pioneer wife or the whore with a heart of gold. Today, the more varied roles of women are being uncovered. In 2006, *Texas Women on the Cattle Trails* was published, including the story of contemporaries of Charles and Fannie who were driving cattle from Texas. I wonder what they would have made of Hattie and George Cluck, who arrived in Abilene, Kansas, a few weeks before the Rices passed through Omaha. George had avoided signing up for the Civil War and started raising cattle in Texas instead. In April 1871, George, Hattie, and their three young children joined another rancher and fourteen men to drive their herds up the Chisholm Trail to Abilene. The trip was long, arduous, and dangerous. Crossing the swiftly flowing Red River on horses was risky, and they were threatened at one point by bandits trying to steal the livestock, but they reached Abilene and successfully sold their stock. This extraordinary story ended with an event that was even more surprising. On the same day that Charles and Fannie were in burned-out Chicago, Hattie was giving birth to their fourth child. She undertook that trip knowing she was pregnant, but dealt with this along with all the external risks. It probably wasn't a choice, just something she had to do.

This story reminded me of Charles and Fannie's experience of having children, atypical for the times. They were married for twelve

*Fannie and Charles' children: Howard (my
grandfather) and Marion (my great aunt).*

years before my grandfather was born. Then they had a daughter four
years later, but no more children. Having only two children is so common now that it took me a while to remember it was unusual back
then, and to wonder why they stopped at two. And why did it take so
long for Fannie to get pregnant? There's no indication that she had
miscarriages. I don't know for sure, but I've concluded that it may not
have been a coincidence that her pregnancy happened shortly after
Charles changed his employment and the two of them moved away
from her family.

When Charles was courting Fannie, he was already working for
her father, Edward Crosby. Edward was a canny entrepreneur, and

had grasped that the grain business was moving out of New England and further west. He secured contracts to buy wheat from the West (initially New York State, then Minnesota) and sell it in the East. He prospered. As part of the discussions about marriage to his daughter, Edward asked Charles to become a partner in his grain milling business, an offer that Charles accepted, joining Fannie's brother, Edward, and her sister Ella's husband, Leroy Adams.

I get the impression from Charles' diaries that his job after marriage involved mostly traveling, selling on the wheat, so he and Fannie were often apart. He never said so, but perhaps he felt that he was being kept firmly under his father-in-law's thumb. In the summer of 1877, when he was thirty-nine, he recorded in his diary (and Fannie recorded in hers) that he was planning to leave his father-in-law's firm, although he gave no reason. A few months later, he had severed his arrangement with Edward Crosby and taken up a partnership with a grain merchant in Worcester, Massachusetts. He and Fannie moved there on December 5, 1877, into rented accommodation. Their son Howard was born about nine months later, on September 16, 1878. Serendipity?

Beyond Laramie, Fannie reported that they saw a herd of buffalo. ("Buffalo" was the term popularly used, though "bison" was the correct term.) These unusual animals were among the impressive sights that train travelers were told to look out for. In 1861, there were up to twelve million buffalo on the Great Plains. However, by 1883, only a few hundred remained. The Rices saw just this one small herd on their trip out to San Francisco. When they returned through Kansas the following spring, an area where buffalo were more common, they saw more herds—but also hundreds of carcasses of dead buffalo. Buffalo were an essential part of Plains Indians' diet and culture, but when white traders arrived, Indians also readily killed the animals to sell the hides in exchange for the brass, iron, glass, and wool products the traders brought.

Later, the transcontinental railroad brought many easterners who enjoyed killing buffalo as sport. (I know Charles enjoyed hunting, because he did some in California, but I'm relieved he wasn't interested in shooting buffalo.) Representatives of the government

*Charles' father-in-law, Edward Crosby, is shown seated,*
*backed by his partners who ran E. Crosby & Company.*
*From left to right: Leroy Adams (Edward's son-in-law),*
*Charles, and Edward Chandler Crosby (Edward's son).*

deliberately sat back and allowed this to happen because they knew it would destroy the Plains Indians' way of life. As an army officer explained it to a buffalo hunter in 1872, "There's no two ways about it: either the buffalo or the Indian must go. Only when the Indian becomes absolutely dependent on us for his every need, will we be able to handle him. He's too independent with the buffalo. But if we kill the buffalo we conquer the Indian. It seems a more humane thing to kill the buffalo than the Indian, so the buffalo must go."

The monstrous slaughter of the buffalo is a story of the West that was barely reported until quite recently—Charles and Fannie were probably unaware of it. Ironically, Buffalo Bill, who played a part in the slaughter in the 1860s when he was under contract to supply Kansas Pacific Railroad workers with buffalo meat, also played a part in the later rescue of the buffalo, ensuring that the animals that participated in his show continued to breed and increase.

Charles and Fannie passed through Rawlins, Wyoming, without comment because it was during the night. I remember Rawlins well from my trip in 1965. Betty and I started talking to a family with four young children while shopping in a supermarket there. They invited us home for dinner and persuaded us to stay the night. Their friendliness and hospitality were among the highlights of our trip. The next day I wrote, "B and I went off to the rodeo—small town and much fun—calf-roping, bronc-riding, bull-riding, and a barrel race. I had a chance to wear my new leather jacket I bought in Landers." I still have that jacket. I never wore it much, so it's in a trunk in the loft, but it remains an important souvenir of that trip out West.

The friendly family recommended a glorious driving route through the high Snowy Range in the Medicine Bow National Forest. I noticed, looking on the internet, that there is now a designated Snowy Range Scenic Byway, with visitor centers at both the eastern and western entrances to the National Forest. I expect it was more fun when we relied on word of mouth and the back roads were empty. On the other hand, on the internet I've learned far more interesting things about the area's history than I did when I was there, such as how the area became known as Medicine Bow. It seems that the Plains Indians went there for mountain mahogany, which produces bows of exceptional quality. Tribes would assemble to construct bows, but also to undertake ceremonies for making medicine, curing diseases, and calling on the Great Spirit.

It led us to Laramie and then to Steamboat Springs and the Fetcher Ranch. After that trip, I was hooked. I decided I would definitely move to the West after college. I went back for my final year in the autumn, met a charming Englishman who hailed from the Lake District, and ended up moving to Britain instead, to marry him.

Occasionally I reflect on that decision, which completely changed the course of my life. Even though I was in love, why was I so willing to leave the country of my birth and move to a foreign country that I had never even been to? I think part of the reason is that my family has a long tradition of links with Britain and Europe. My grandfather, instead of going to college, traveled through Europe in 1897. In 1932, my parents went to Europe for their honeymoon, and they particularly loved the English Lake District, home to so many literary figures they admired. My uncle, after teaching in France in the 1930s, came back with a French wife. When I was eleven, I joined that tradition by living with family friends in Italy for nine months to learn Italian at school. To top it off, it seems that when my mother met my English boyfriend, she secretly had me married off to him and living in the Lake District long before it ever occurred to me!

I have never regretted my decision. Britain is my home: it feels like home, and I have dual nationality. But I'm also American, so I'm delighted that retirement has given me an opportunity to reconnect with my childhood hopes and dreams. Belonging to two countries is becoming more and more common in this globalized world, although some would like to turn the clock back. Not me. I have begun to feel that I belong to global Earth, not this or that nation state.

---

THE RICES' BREAKFAST the next day at Bryan (now a ghost town) in western Wyoming "did not deserve the name," said Fannie. Charles wrote: "We breakfasted at Bryan, and a most contemptible meal it was. Everything was filthy and nothing was cooked. One dollar was the price and the landlord was cheeky enough to say to someone who made some complaint 'that as many praised his table as found fault.' What a blessing to have cheek!" I can almost feel Charles' irritation, and would soon feel it myself as I approached Salt Lake City. The high open ranges of Wyoming cross the state boundary into Utah and then to the escarpment of the Wasatch Range, where the railroad makes a rapid drop of several thousand feet through zigzagging valleys and canyons on the approach to Ogden. Charles reported that the descent was "at a fearful rate," plunging into Echo Canyon and past the famous "One Thousand Mile Tree" standing forlornly as a milestone, a thousand miles west of Omaha.

Crofutt's guide described the milestone in more extravagant Victorian style:

"This living milestone of nature's planning has long marked this place; long before the hardy Mormon passed down this wild gorge; long before the great transcontinental railroad was even thought of. It stood a lonely sentinel, when all around was desolation; when the lurking savage and wild beast claimed supremacy, and each in turn reposed in the shade of its waving arms. How changed the scene! The ceaseless bustle of an active, progressive age, the hum of labor, the roar and rush of the passing locomotive has usurped the old quiet, and henceforward the lone tree will be, not a guide to the gloomy past, but an index of the coming greatness of a regenerated country."

I think Charles and Fannie would have agreed with this sentiment, but it evokes in me a stab of irony and a feeling of sadness at this romantic glorification of progress. I have since read that the lone tree died, but was replaced. It is in a defile with no houses or old roads, but has the unused railroad, the river, and Interstate 84 to keep it company.

I was envious of my great-grandparents. They came on the original railroad route along the Weber River as it runs through spectacular scenery to Ogden. That line was closed to train traffic in 1997, and a group of rail enthusiasts have been campaigning ever since for it to be reopened. I approached Salt Lake City from Colorado through Provo, with no views of mountains or any other scenery because it was the middle of the night. I was irritable, and had snapped at one of the train crew who paid no attention to my request that she speak more clearly. I was also fed up because the train was nearly four hours late. Despite the 1973 Amtrak law that gave priority to passenger trains, bully-boy freight trains push to the front all the time. I agree heartily with Tom Zoellner, a San Francisco academic and author of *Train: Riding the Rails That Created the Modern World,* who said, "Though freight railroads might holler and cry poverty, it is time to uphold the law and recognize that passenger rights trump Big Coal and Big Oil."

# 5

# SALT LAKE CITY
# AND THE MORMONS

*October 25, 1871. Words fail me when trying to describe*
*the canyons. The whole afternoon we passed through*
*fine scenery. Reached Salt Lake City at 8:00 p.m. tired*
*and sleepy. Two of our car friends went with us.*

—Fannie's diary

WHEN I fell in love with the West, I decided Colorado and Wyoming were my favorite states. With their ranches, rodeos, historic trails, and ghost towns, they were redolent of cowboy and frontier stories. So being diverted from Charles and Fannie's route wasn't really a hardship, because the Colorado Rocky Mountain scenery brought back fond memories of Betty's and my visit to the Fetcher Ranch and our oxygen-starved explorations of the high mountain passes in my VW beetle. The rest of the Rices' trip was through Utah, Nevada, and California, which I didn't remember with the same nostalgia, but these areas of the West still included Indians and cowboys, so I was looking forward to discovering new differences from the Wild West of my imagination. Meanwhile, I was rejoining Charles and Fannie's route of 1871, and they made a point of stopping for nearly a week in Salt Lake City, where the Mormons had arrived in 1847 and begun their own very different story of settling the West.

To understand the Mormons, I needed to work out where they fit into the history of religion in America. The First Amendment of the US Constitution in 1789 guaranteed freedom of worship and forbade the government from interfering in religion. A radical experiment in governance at the time, it opened the gates to a ferment of interpreting the Bible. During what is called the Second Great Awakening, between the 1790s and 1830s, Protestant religious revival spread all over the country, bringing converts to some existing denominations and leading to the formation of five new ones. One of these was the Church of Jesus Christ of Latter-day Saints (or the LDS Church), founded in 1830 by Joseph Smith with the publication of the Book of Mormon, the sacred text for the new religion.

When I first began reading about the Mormons, I found reams of prejudiced anti-Mormon material, which I put to the side. I also found modern, well-researched, and evidence-based histories that I have relied on to help me understand Mormon history. It is complex, and in this account I am bound to oversimplify, but I hope to remain as objective as possible.

Unlike other religious groups, the LDS Church went out on a limb, claiming its followers were the chosen people who must build Zion, the Kingdom of God, on earth. This was more than a set of beliefs; it was work to be done together, and it meant control of a geographical area and of the character of its society. (The same concept can be said to apply to Israel, with the assertion of a divine right to all of Palestine by militant Zionists.) Joseph Smith led a growing group of converts from New York to Ohio, to Missouri, and to Illinois, trying to establish Zion. The fact that the Mormons had a political structure, not just a church structure, clashed with the national principle of the separation of church and state, and also created conflict with the non-Mormons living in the same area. Convinced of their divine entitlement, the Mormons heard revelations announced from the pulpit and voted in local elections as a block, which could give them a majority over non-Mormons. In Illinois—the location of their third attempt to establish Zion—they bought the land surrounding the town of Commerce with church funds, renamed it Nauvoo, and secured a charter to set up courts and a militia. The anger of the non-Mormons escalated, and in 1844 a mob murdered Joseph Smith.

Brigham Young, the most senior of the Twelve Apostles at the head of the church, became the new leader. Joseph Smith had been inspiring and charismatic; Young's skills were more practical—he could get things done. He realized that building Zion without conflict would require a location that was exceedingly remote, and he identified the semi-arid basin of the Great Salt Lake, a thousand miles away in the far north of Mexico, as a good choice, saying it was "a point where a good living will require hard labor and consequently will be coveted by no other people, while it is surrounded by so unpopulous but fertile a country." What leaps out at me is that he ignored the presence of Indians.

By the time the Mormons got to the Great Basin in 1847, it had been removed from Mexico and annexed by America, and there were plans to build the transcontinental railroad through it. It was no longer remote, but the creation of the Mormon nation under the authority of Brigham Young began. Their achievements in this inhospitable region of the Great Basin were remarkable. A tightly controlled church hierarchy set everyone to work irrigating the land so that they could farm productively, a technique completely foreign to American pioneers. The Mormon leadership instituted a strict regime of tithing to ensure that no one would be abandoned to poverty, and they extolled hard work and discipline, soon offering tangible proof that it would be rewarded with property. The arrangements gave people security in a time of enormous change. I can understand why it was so appealing.

On arrival in the Great Basin, the Mormons had formed a provisional state called Deseret, whose boundaries included most of the annexed Mexican land, and they petitioned for US statehood. The federal government instead established a much smaller Territory of Utah, but appointed Brigham Young as governor. The religious structure of Mormonism could be described as a theocracy and Brigham Young's authority appeared to be absolute, verging on dictatorship. Although, as a group, they had substantially different characteristics from conventional pioneers settling the West, they were still operating in the western frontier environment of lawlessness that existed before federal structures were set up. Convinced they were doing the will of God, Young and the Mormons established their own rule of law. It seems to me that their rule of law was similar to what in other parts of western America was called vigilantism.

Polygamy as a practice had been rumored for many years and was finally made official in 1852. It wasn't practiced widely, because only the men with enough money could support more than one wife, but this conduct was considered beyond the pale by many Americans, making them receptive to the widespread negative stories about these "peculiar people." It also created much interest, and from 1869 the Mormon settlement was readily accessible by train so that curious transcontinental tourists like my great-grandparents could come and have a look.

As their train hurtled down the Weber Valley, approaching Utah, Charles wrote of seeing a Mormon settlement with long adobe houses having many doors, indicating, in his assessment, that "Mr. Mormon had many wives." In his next comment, I am sure he was being facetious. He wrote, "As we neared the city a smell of sulphur arose and had it not been explained we might have considered it as ominous, and have expected to find the city being visited by a 'rain of fire and brimstone' from heaven on account of its wickedness, like Sodom of old. We found that the odor arose from some hot sulphur springs near the road and even in the darkness could see the steam rising like a mist from them. Reaching the city we resolved to give the Mormon hotel a wide berth and therefore put up at the Salt Lake House" (whose proprietors were Gentiles—as the Mormons called non-Mormons then).

I was feeling decidedly cross on my approach to Salt Lake City because it was 2:30 A.M., but I was greeted with such a friendly welcome that all my touchiness vanished. Mary Rollo, my Affordable Travel Club host, seemed genuinely unconcerned that I had arrived at such an early hour, just saying that the Amtrak station was in an area where I shouldn't be out after dark. Salt Lake City is big (with a population of 190,000), and we seemed to drive for ages to get to her condominium in the south of the city. The next morning we got acquainted, and discovered that apart from religion (she is a practicing Mormon), we had a lot in common and plenty to talk about. I was surprised and delighted that she was also an Obama supporter.

I had visited Salt Lake City with my family in 1963, but I had no memory of that visit except for an image of some wide stone steps leading up to an impressive building. I have reread the articles that my father (John Hooper, the editor of the *Brattleboro Daily Reformer*) sent back describing our trip, and he says that before we went into Salt Lake City, we went for a swim in the Great Salt Lake. I had completely forgotten this, but reading the article made a vivid memory pop into my head, of bobbing about like toy ducks in water that seemed much too salty. After the swim, we went to the famous daily organ recital in the Tabernacle, requested by our organ-playing friend who was traveling with us. Unlike Chicago and Omaha, historic Salt Lake City is well-preserved, and it is possible to see many of the same buildings my great-grandparents saw, although some of them were still under construction when the Rices visited.

Charles and Fannie awoke refreshed the morning after their arrival in Salt Lake City and went out for a walk before breakfast. Charles was most interested in the layout of the city, describing standing on high ground and seeing a nearly level plain spread out to the south, with the River Jordan flowing through it. He even listed detailed measurements. As for me, I couldn't stop looking at the stupendous mountains. They erupt from the edges of the city's plain, forming a rocky and often snow-covered rampart of pinnacles to the north and the east, but they are far enough away not to crowd the city. They provide a striking backdrop. It's not surprising we had such different perceptions. I love mountains—looking at them and exploring them. Charles, on the contrary, felt that cities and urban development were novel and interesting. Different individuals, different times.

After breakfast, Charles and Fannie called on Mrs. Richardson, the Mormon sister of one of their Brattleboro friends, and then Mr. Lamb, another friend of a friend. Following their social calls, they went to the hot springs they had smelled from the train, where Charles had a bath, finding it invigorating (in water he noted as 102° F). Perhaps he was also hoping it would help his war wound, which sometimes flared up with infection; he went for another bath the following day. These hot springs provided bathing for city residents until 1946, when the high bacteria count was noticed. Sulphur and chlorine don't mix, so the baths were closed until the spring waters could be diverted to provide private bathing and the public got chlorinated tap water. In 1976, they closed for good, but the vaguely Spanish-looking building remained. It is now derelict, and can still be seen from the train on the line between Ogden and Salt Lake City.

Charles and Fannie rested in the afternoon and in the evening

*I remember Wells Fargo stagecoaches from my childhood image of
the Wild West, so I was delighted to find myself cycling in to use the
drive-in cash dispenser at a Wells Fargo Bank in Salt Lake City.*

went to Salt Lake City Theatre, built in 1861. This frontier town
aspired to culture. They saw a performance by a Japanese troupe that
Charles said was "a poor affair." Mrs. Richardson returned their call
two days later, when Charles and Fannie were out, and Fannie, with
her usual obscurity, wrote, "We returned her call and had a funny
experience."

I was glad to get my bike reassembled after such a long time on
the train, and cycled into the city center from Mary's condo. When
the city was being built, Brigham Young decreed that the main streets
should be wide enough for a team of oxen and a covered wagon to
turn around "without profanity," so they are 132 feet wide. That pre-
scient ruling means that the streets are wide enough to accommodate
parking, cycle lanes, and two lanes of traffic on both sides of a central median, with ample space for sidewalks in front of the house lots.
Used to the cramped conditions of British streets, which are often
barely wide enough for a car to pass a bike, I found myself cheering
with delight.

*Some teenage boys enjoy showing off their homemade raised-seat bikes outside the public library in Salt Lake City.*

The city website had told me I could get a map of cycle lanes from the City and County Building. I found it and went in, but there was no reception desk, just a directory of where offices were and a long corridor. I chose Policy and Development, walked into that office, and still saw no reception desk. I wandered around and saw some people at a table. I asked if they were having a meeting, and they said yes, to which I replied, "I'm sorry, but I'm from England, and I was told I could get a cycle map here. Can you direct me to the right office?" One of the men said, "It's two feet behind you." I turned around, and a woman handed me the cycle map. I was tickled by the informality of this western city government.

Back outside, I was treated to a performance by some young urban cyclists who had altered their bikes. The saddles were up on stalks with pedals, about six feet higher than usual. Four of them weaved and swooped around the pedestrianized area, displaying their prowess to the bystanders.

During their visit to Salt Lake City, Charles and Fannie tried to see Brigham Young on two occasions, each time being told he wasn't available and leaving their card. I made a beeline to Beehive House, where they must have gone because it's where Young worked and lived. I looked around his office, visualizing my great-grandparents standing there 137 years ago and talking to Young's secretary. I tried to think of reasons why a young couple passing through the Mormon capital thought they might be received by the church leader. Could it have been the Vermont connection? Brigham Young was born in Whitingham, a Vermont village about twenty-five miles west of Brattleboro. Brigham Young's family came to Whitingham just before Brigham was born, and moved on to New York State when he was three, so it's unlikely the Rices knew someone who knew the Youngs. Perhaps they just thought it was worth chancing their luck. It does strike me as out of character, and I wish I knew why they kept trying.

My tour guides to Young's home were two young Mormons from Brazil and the Far East, whose narrative was all about what a marvelous family man he was. Modern Mormons don't accept polygamy, so perhaps that's why they didn't mention that he had fifty-five wives and fifty-seven children. He had the Lion House added to the Beehive House to provide extra living space. Walking through the handsome rooms full of beautiful nineteenth-century furnishings, I was struck by how sumptuously he had lived in the frontier West.

My father, in one of the columns sent to his newspaper, wrote about the many Vermont possessions he had seen in a museum; both the first president of the church, Joseph Smith, and Brigham Young were born in Vermont. I have always been rather taken with this Vermont connection, as possibly Charles and Fannie were. I think other Vermonters are, too. About a hundred years ago, persons unknown erected a stone slab on the site where Young was born. The epigraph read, "Brigham Young Born on This Spot 1801—A Man of Much Courage and Superb Equipment." (This stone, much-quoted by people making fun of the Mormons, has since disappeared.)

The question of whether or not Brigham Young might have received Charles and Fannie was eclipsed the following day by my discovery of the news that he was busy avoiding arrest. I had some information from their diaries, but not the broader context, so to find out more about what exactly was happening in October 1871, I sought out the Central Library. It was the most extraordinary library I had ever been in—it's made mostly of glass, so the spectacular Wasatch Mountains are constantly present outside the windows. How do people concentrate? The sensational sights beckoned, and I decided to read about Mormonism later.

Temple Square, which includes the houses built for Young, is of great symbolic importance to Mormons. When the Rices visited, the Temple was still under construction, and it wasn't finished until 1893. Charles was most impressed with the unusually shaped Tabernacle, recording numerous details about what was under the dome and how it was designed to prevent the sun heating it up too much in the summer. He couldn't resist a dig at the Mormons when he observed their Tithing House, where Mormons brought a tenth of their year's earnings to support the church. He wrote, "Undoubtedly 'the Church' in reality is Brigham Young and his fellow leaders of this horde of deluded people, who labor hard year by year and without one word of complaint render an honest account of their year's income, sincerely believing that their leaders are as honest as they."

When I visited it was a cloudless day. The Tabernacle and the Temple shimmered in the sun, surrounded by gardens with vividly colored flowers creating reflections on the pools and fountains being fed by City Creek. I stopped to admire one of the pools that magically reflected the Temple spires against the blue sky, all framed by the flowers. Mormon wedding parties were everywhere, posing for photographs.

Leaving the central part of the city, I cycled northwards up Capitol Hill to the historic Marmalade District. Its steep streets have names like Almond, Vine, Apricot, and Quince, reflecting the first residents, who planted fruit and nut trees. The clapboard houses are modest-sized, but built in a plethora of Victorian architectural styles and painted in an array of shades. I stopped to take a photo of a telephone pole swathed to the top with the green leaves and orangey-red flowers of a trumpet vine that had spread out from a nearby garden.

Coming back down the hill, I went past the McCune Mansion, a late Victorian extravaganza built by mining and railroad tycoon

*The Temple of the Church of the Latter-Day Saints
is reflected in a pool in Salt Lake City.*

Alfred McCune in 1900, for a million dollars. It is now used for posh events such as wedding receptions, and is said to be haunted by benign ghosts. As I turned away from photographing the mansion, I did a double take and tried to identify what I was seeing. Down the hill below me, a forest appeared to be growing up the side of a

large building. It turned out to be the north side of the new Conference Center built for the Church of Latter-day Saints, which has ter-
racing projecting from the walls and planted with pine trees. It also
has a prairie on the roof and a waterfall cascading down the front of
the building from a rooftop spire (fed by and recycled from a spring
underneath the building). City Creek has been uncovered and flows
through the site on its way to the Jordan River. The landscaping is
meant to echo the mountains and meadows of Utah while not detracting from the Temple and the Tabernacle across the road. Perhaps they
are trying to make up for the dreadful 1960s skyscraper that looms
over the Temple and contains the bureaucracy for the church's nearly
fourteen million members worldwide and its missionary work.

Not far west of the LDS Conference Center, I was startled to come
across a noisy motocross competition happening in a walled-off lot,
with motorbike riders launching themselves off steep ramps to per-
form amazing acrobatics up in the air, accompanied by an excited
loudspeaker commentary. What on earth was this doing in downtown
Salt Lake City? No one looking over the wall from the street outside
could tell me, so I wandered back into Temple Square, passing a beg-
gar who sat with a sign and a bowl in front of him. The sign said:
"Homeless Mormon trying to get back on my feet. God bless all you
fine people." Clever marketing skills, I thought. Mary later said it was
a good spot for beggars because people coming out of a service were
definitely more inclined to be charitable.

I then went in search of the Amshack and the bad area that Mary
had made sure I didn't have to cycle through, reckoning it was daytime and I would notice if things started to look too rough. It wasn't
rough where I went, and I found myself in the middle of a celebration
of Mexico's Independence Day, September 16. I had enjoyed a visit
to Mexico years earlier and wondered what the members of its dias-
pora were up to, so I joined the audience in front of an outdoor stage
and watched the lively Mexican Hat Dance being performed by two
couples: the women twirling in ruffled full skirts in the colors of the
Mexican flag—red, green, and white—and the men in skintight black
and white mariachi outfits with red bandanas around their necks and
enormous sombreros. I felt like I was back in Mexico, until I noticed

the banners of the sponsoring organizations. One was "Zion Bank—We know who keeps us in business."

It was finally dawning on me that Salt Lake City, although founded by the Mormons and the headquarters of the Church of Latter-day Saints, is not all Mormon. I learned that fewer than half the residents are Mormon, and a fifth are of Central or South American origin. It is a cosmopolitan and multiethnic city, with crime, drug problems, and gangs in some low-income districts. The Amtrak Station is near Pioneer Park, which apparently is used for drug dealing and perhaps truly is not a place for a cyclist alone in the middle of the night. In the state of Utah as a whole, however, Mormons are still in the majority (although the percentage is going down). The state's politics are conservative Republican, whereas Salt Lake City's politics are Democratic.

On the Saturday of their stay, Charles and Fannie made their second visit to Brigham Young, who was "still away." They saw Daniel Wells, the mayor, looking very agitated, and someone told them Wells had been arrested on a charge of murder. Murder! That prompted the couple to seek out the federal court in the afternoon to see what was happening. Charles wrote, "So bitter is the feeling of the Mormons toward the General Government that they will not allow the United States Court to hold its sessions in the Territorial Mormon Court House, and at the time of our visit, the Court was being held in a large barnlike room over a livery stable, the rooms being strongly impregnated with horse."

The federal judge, James McKean, was presiding, and Daniel Wells was brought in. Charles wrote, "His face is of the villainous type, indicating craft and cunning." Judge McKean, on the other hand, met with Charles' approval. "In Judge McKean the Government has an agent fearless and at the same time impartial and just—a Christian gentleman." I wonder if Charles' judgment could have been influenced by McKean having been born in Vermont and having serving as a colonel in the Civil War. At 5:00 P.M. a warrant for Brigham Young's arrest was also issued, but he couldn't be found, apparently having gotten wind of it and leaving town.

I discovered that Charles and Fannie's visit to the Mormon capital coincided with one of the crunch points in the long saga of the US government's battle to assert its authority over the Mormons. In 1857, there had nearly been a war when US troops were sent to quell a supposed rebellion. That ended with a compromise, with Brigham Young stepping down as governor and a federal appointee put in his place. The Mormon leadership then simply ran a shadow government alongside the federal authority. In 1871, the Utah Territory was on its eighth non-Mormon governor, George Lemuel Woods, whose federal authority continued to be ignored. James McKean was appointed Chief Justice of Utah Territory and came on an anti-Mormon mission. In the 1857 conflict, Bill Hickman had murdered a trader because he was trading with the US army instead of the Mormons, and confessed to this in 1871, saying it had been on the orders of the Mormon leadership. This explains why Wells was arrested and the authorities also sought to arrest Brigham Young. But Hickman's confession wasn't backed up with other evidence, and McKean was unable to get convictions.

I was intrigued by the historic center of the city, but the mountain scenery enticed me away. On the cycle map, something called Canyon Road seemed to be the nearest way into the mountains, and it looked especially appealing because there was no housing. I set off through the heart of the city, which quickly gave way to a neighborhood of small houses surrounded by mature trees and flowers. Canyon Road was normal-sized, not 132 feet wide. On the western side was a strip of woodland with a small creek flowing through it, carefully confined in a curving stone channel that continued under the cross streets. I wondered if it was one of the channels of water that Charles had remarked on approvingly, which came from the melting snows in the mountains down the canyons to the city, and then flowed into ditches along the streets, which he noted "were bordered with cottonwood, locust, balm of Gilead and box elder shade trees."

Beyond the houses, I found myself in a spacious canyon with scattered scrubby trees and golden waving grasses rising up steeply on each side, and the creek running down the middle. Lots of cyclists were on the road. I looked at my watch and realized they were probably out for an after-work spin. We were in unspoiled countryside, just a ten-minute cycle from the busy city center. The road went up one side of the creek and then did a dogleg to come back on the other side higher up, providing a panoramic view of the city, the mountains, and the imposing Utah State Capitol building, near the foot of the ravine.

I had happened upon an important part of the city's history. City Creek was the basis of the water system that Charles described. The centralized organization of the Latter-day Saints meant that the creek and its watershed were protected right from the beginning, unlike in so many other places where an individualistic free-for-all prevailed over the common good. Brigham Young established a system of land and water distribution, knowing that their community's existence depended on agriculture and water. No land was to be bought or sold, but must be given to the LDS Church as an inheritance. All the land in the watershed is city- or federally owned. A water treatment plant was built in the 1950s and City Creek still supplies a portion of the city, including the Temple fountains and gardens.

I was enjoying cycling gradually upward on the road along the bottom of the canyon when I recognized from a jolt and a thud that I had a flat tire. My heart sank like the tire when I took in that it was my rear tire, and the wrench I needed for taking the nut off the wheel fixture (not a quick release) was back at Mary's condo. At least there were plenty of cyclists around, so I started asking each one who passed if she or he had a wrench. A woman cyclist said no, but gave me her cell phone number to ring if I didn't have things sorted out in an hour. Another cyclist said no, but pumped up my tire, which only lasted a few minutes. Eventually, a young man said he had a wrench in his car, parked further down the road. He left me with the first woman, who had generously come back to see how I was getting on, and she escorted me to his car while he cycled to his house nearby to leave his bike and walk back to his car. Phew!

The young man and I set about changing the tire, but neither of us could work out how to get the Bike Friday's unusual hub gear gizmo off, so he insisted on giving me and my bike a lift back to Mary's condo, in faraway south Salt Lake City. He was an environmental engineer from St. Louis, and since he and his wife were both

Mormons, they had decided to move to Salt Lake City. He drove us through the historic center to show me the Temple and the Tabernacle with pride, and then to the suburbs, where we stopped at a bike shop, unfortunately about to close. It was dark by the time he dropped me off at the condo. What a nice guy!

I was exhausted and felt very much in need of a glass of wine with my meal. I had bought food at a supermarket for my dinner, but in Mormon Utah, alcohol is only sold at state liquor stores. Mary insisted on driving me out to a liquor store to buy my wine.

The next morning, with the help of my Bike Friday manual, I changed the tire, but then I couldn't get the hub gear to work. Mary dropped my bike and me off at a nearby bike shop, where they adjusted my hub gear and didn't charge me anything. So many people were going so far out of their way to help me—I was touched to get such a welcome in this big city.

The next-to-last day of Charles and Fannie's visit was a Sunday, so of course they went to church. In the morning they went to a Presbyterian Church, Charles commenting that the Reverend Mr. Welch was having difficulty organizing a church among the Saints. They were introduced to Governor Wood and the Indian agent, no doubt getting the federal government gossip on the nefarious doings of the Mormon leaders. In the afternoon they went to the service at the Tabernacle, along with four thousand Mormons, to hear Orson Pratt preach. Charles wrote that Pratt gave his sermon on the biblical basis for polygamy and the villainy of the federal attacks on Mormons. He cited David and Solomon as examples of prominent men in Bible history who had many wives and yet pleased God, and claimed that polygamy was a right and a part of the Mormon religion, and that the number of wives a Mormon should have was a matter of conscience.

Charles went on: "He then abused the United States Officers of the Territory in a most violent manner. Seemingly there was not language strong enough to express his hatred and contempt of them. Said he was ready to stand suits at law and suffer the penalty, even to imprisonment for twenty years, but could pay no fines as he was poor." Charles had been told that Orson Pratt was the only Mormon leader who hadn't made a fortune off the people, but he was a fanatic and a tool of the more crafty ones. After expressing disgust at more speeches by other prominent leaders, Charles concluded: "There were some 4,000 Mormons gathered to listen to such haranguing. When we gazed about over the audience and measured the mental capacity of the people congregated, we were not surprised that they had been duped and led in the way they have been traveling for so many years." Charles' comment about low intelligence in Mormons and his description of Mayor Wells having a villainous face made me wince. Again, however, he was reflecting mainstream views about the Mormons, and what we now regard as defamatory language seems to have been the norm in the 1870s. Fannie probably best summarizes what she and Charles thought about their contact with these people: "The day has been very strange."

They witnessed the height of the clash between the federal government and the Mormons, when strong feelings were aroused and the government was trying but failing to assert its authority. In the years after that, it fell to non-Mormons and Mormons within Utah to undertake a slower process of negotiating a solution to the clash of church and state. In 1890, the president of the church officially renounced polygamy, paving the way to official statehood for Utah in 1896. (This rejection of polygamy was not accepted by some Mormons, and many polygamous Mormon sects were formed and are still thriving today—but that's another story.)

On my last day in Salt Lake City, I initiated a conversation with Mary about her Mormon beliefs. My ancestors were mainstream Protestant. My mother, granddaughter of Congregationalist Charles and Fannie, grew up a Congregationalist, but when she married my father, she joined his Unitarian Church. So I grew up Unitarian.

Unitarianism is a liberal denomination that uses all the world's religious traditions and prophets as sources of inspiration and truth. It's where I developed my ethical framework. The only "creed" I can remember is the Golden Rule: "Do unto others as you would have others do unto you." (I learned it with that wording, not a modern version.) Sometimes I say I am an atheist, because I definitely don't believe in a supernatural entity that knows what I and everyone else is thinking or doing, but other times I say I am an agnostic, because I think many atheists are arrogant in their certainty that there is no God as a result of a lack of scientific evidence. There is so much we humans still don't know, so I keep an open mind. Meanwhile, I value compassion and concern for others, I campaign for justice and equality, and I believe that I have an obligation to try to make a positive difference while I'm here on this earth.

Trying to understand Mary's position, I summoned up the courage (or nerve) to ask her whether she really believed that Joseph Smith dug up some gold tablets in New York State that were a revelation from God. She said, "Yes, I definitely do. The Lord was telling Joseph Smith to go back to the beginnings of Jesus' teaching." Mary, a highly educated retired teacher, explained it thus: "We all have a rational side and a spiritual side. When I'm trying to make a decision, I weigh up all the rational reasons, but I also consult the Lord, and I look for feelings of peace within myself to know the right decision."

With my background, I can't comprehend making an "act of faith," so I didn't know how to continue the conversation with Mary. I'm afraid I changed the subject. However, I think I have a spiritual side, too. I would call it my soul—but it's about feelings and relationships with others, and wonder and awe at the natural world, not a relationship with God. Maybe I should read that book *Beyond Religion* that I had seen in the Soul Desires bookstore in Omaha.

Charles and Fannie's diaries reflect the ambivalence that Mormonism evoked (and still evokes) in observers. They were horrified by polygamy and the Mormon leaders, but they admired the obvious hard work and the well-ordered productive farmland that showed how the Mormons were clearly achieving the shared goals of American progress and development. I responded to the heartwarming generosity and kindness of the Mormons I met, but I still had serious questions about what the LDS Church does with its enormous wealth, and about its hierarchical all-male ruling structure.

So where were the American Indians during this titanic undertaking? When the Mormons arrived in 1847, fewer than twenty thousand Utes and Shoshone lived in the areas being settled, many having died from disease since the first contact with whites. The Book of Mormon and Joseph Smith taught that the Indians were descended from Israelite peoples who had migrated to the American continent shortly before the destruction of Jerusalem and the Babylonian captivity. These benighted descendants could be saved and brought into God's Latter-day Kingdom.

Brigham Young sent out missionaries and had some success, but practical dealings were influenced more by Euro-American attitudes. The Indians felt the Mormons were invading their territory and thought it fair to exact a tax in cattle, clothing, and other possessions, which the Mormons perceived as stealing. The Mormons tried to get the federal government to buy the land from the Indians, but in the meantime they simply moved in and converted Indian hunting and gathering lands and farmlands into family farms and ranches. Violent clashes were not uncommon.

When I started this journey, I knew hardly anything up to date about American Indians. I had read Dee Brown's *Bury My Heart at Wounded Knee: An Indian History of the American West* (1987), but that was it. The trip was bringing home to me how varied the tribes and cultures are, and the huge amount I didn't know. When I was in grade school, I can remember wondering about Indians who had lived in Vermont before white settlers came. Had they lived in the woods around my house? What I found out left me with the belief that early Indians had traveled through Vermont mainly along the Connecticut River, but didn't live there, and that when my ancestors, who were the first white settlers in Dover, Vermont, came along, all the Indians had been driven to Canada by the French and Indian Wars of the 1760s.

I decided to learn about that history, so I read *The Western Abenakis of Vermont* (1994) by Colin Calloway. Like Limerick's book, it was a revelation. My understanding that Indians only passed through Vermont was wrong. They moved from place to place depending on the seasons and food availability, but they returned to those same places, including a settlement on the banks of the Connecticut River, just south of Brattleboro. And they didn't all go to Canada. Small groups hung on here and there, living on the fringes of white communities. I feel angry but also sad that I didn't know any of this when I was growing up. It would have enriched my understanding of the area's history and shown me the other side of the heroic story I was taught. When I was in touch with some friends in Brattleboro, I was glad to hear that a teacher of 8th graders there was making sure his modern youngsters do learn both sides.

I recognize that the settlement by Mormons of what became the state of Utah gave the area a markedly different history from the rest of the western states. The Mormons' communal vision contrasted with the individualistic outlook of most settlers. Apart from their pioneering journey westward from Illinois to settle the land, Mormons hardly figured in my childhood history books. I hoped the last leg of our train journey across Nevada and into California would return us to the mainstream western story.

At the end of my last day, my lovely host Mary left me at the Amtrak Station at ten P.M., with the train due around eleven P.M. It came in three hours later. I couldn't check in my bike, either, for some reason the railroad personnel couldn't explain. I was fortunate that another passenger volunteered to carry my bagged bike to my coach.

Charles and Fannie left Salt Lake City for the final leg of their journey to San Francisco, expressing pleasure that they had been able to secure a whole sleeping car together with their train friends, Mr. and Mrs. Pelton and their daughter Nellie, Mrs. Whitman, and Mr. Hanna. Charles recorded that the bill at Salt Lake House was thirty dollars (582 dollars in today's money) for five days, at three dollars each per day.

# 6

# ACROSS THE DESERT TO SAN FRANCISCO

*October 31, 1871. The scenery has been dull but new, we
took breakfast at Elko and supper at Humboldt where there
was a fountain and gold fish in the middle of the desert.*
—Fannie's diary

THE TRANSCONTINENTAL railroad was run by two companies.
From Omaha to Salt Lake City, the Union Pacific Railroad was in
charge. The Central Pacific Railroad took over for the remaining journey to California. On the Central Pacific train they joined, Charles
and Fannie obtained a section of a Silver Palace sleeping car for themselves and their new friends. Fannie simply recorded that she preferred the Pullmans on the previous train, but another traveler was
more detailed in her criticism.

Therese Yelverton wrote, "I met with no silver whatever. . . . The
fittings are of the white metal called pinchbeck or Britannia metal."
She complained that they had to go to bed in their boots, "and indeed
ladies cannot undress at all because they cannot shroud themselves
behind the curtains without placing themselves in a recumbent position. Besides, what could be done with their clothing? It could only be
put in the bed and already stowed away there are hand bags, books,
umbrellas, galoshes, wraps, tins of biscuits and possibly a large flask
of Bourbon."

I remembered the earlier remarks of an attendant on my train,
when I had discovered that all the two-person roomettes in the sleeper
cars were fully booked, many by passengers traveling alone. I had
asked the attendant why it wasn't possible for me to share with one
of them. He laughed uproariously. "What? Strangers sharing a bedroom? I don't think this country is ready for that!" I could have told

him about all the strangers, both men and women, sharing an American sleeper car in the 1870s.

Surprisingly, Robert Louis Stevenson found a big improvement in the emigrant cars of the new railroad company. "The cars on the Central Pacific were nearly twice as high, and so proportionally airier; they were freshly varnished, which gave us all a sense of cleanliness as though we had bathed; the seats drew out and joined in the center, so that there was no more need for bed boards; and there was an upper tier of berths which could be closed by day and opened at night."

I left Salt Lake City in the dark, but I don't think I was missing much. On this stretch, even spin master Crofutt was struggling: "All is desolate in the extreme. . ." We had left Utah and were in Nevada, the driest American state, much of it desert and mountains. Beyond the salty barren wastes west of Salt Lake City, however, there are some stunningly beautiful landscapes. This is the traditional home of the Paiute, Shoshone, Washoe, Goshute, and Mohave Indians, who lived sustainably in the harsh desert environment as hunter-gatherers. The arid climate has always been fundamental to how the area has developed and how its people have interacted.

Like many others traveling across Nevada to California, I felt I was just passing through. Even the Nevada Historical Society admits that "Nevada has been on the way to somewhere else for thousands of years." The train route follows the 330 miles of the Humboldt River, a natural corridor across the Great Basin to the foothills of the Sierra Nevada, which mark the boundary with California. It was the path the Washoe Indians used to move into the mountains for the summer season, and the route followed by explorer John C. Frémont and his party in 1844. It was also the path of the old wagon road that the ill-fated Donner Party took to get to California in the winter of 1846–47. Then it became the route of the transcontinental railroad in 1869 and the Victory Highway for motor cars in 1925, which was designated US 40 and then replaced by Interstate 80 in the 1970s—a long-standing natural route to California and the Pacific coast.

Nevada first became a destination for white travelers when gold was discovered in 1849, near the present town of Dayton, 140 miles east of the discovery a year earlier in California. The land was in the

Utah Territory and, in 1850, Mormons established a trading post for prospectors en route to California, then sent more Mormon settlers. By 1856, the Utah territorial government (controlled by Mormons) had established formal control of the area. Gentiles who had started arriving when gold and silver were discovered did not want to be controlled by the Mormons. Disputes and petitions to the government concluded with Nevada being separated from the Mormons' Utah Territory, and Nevada statehood speedily followed, in 1864. The US government kept chipping away at the Utah Territory, so that when the Mormons finally gained statehood for Utah in 1896, the state was only slightly more than a third the size of the original territory.

After the surface gold finds were taken, heavy machinery, capital, and technical expertise were required, so mining was quickly taken over by large companies. Mark Twain lived in Nevada mining areas from 1861 to 1867 and wrote about his experiences in his book *Roughing It* (1872). Mining is still important to Nevada's economy, but it tends to be an unreliable boom-and-bust industry, so there has always been a pressing need to diversify. In the 1920s, the state opened up to the "sin industries" not available elsewhere—prostitution, gambling, prizefighting, and the granting of easy divorces and quick marriages. The glittering Las Vegas Strip in the southeast corner of the state has offered gambling and entertainment since the 1930s, and is one of the most popular destinations for tourists in the United States and the world. Tourism in the scenic parts of the state was also promoted early on, and continues to grow.

Ranching began in Nevada to provide food for the miners, but is still important. Nevada's proximity to California, rather than to Texas, has always influenced its cattle business, so Spanish vaqueros became "buckaroos" and usually are still called that, rather than cowboys. Since the first phase of settlement, however, ranching has been almost entirely controlled by a few large corporations, several dozen families, and the federal government, which still owns 85 percent of the land because it was not conducive to homesteading.

Scarcity of water kept people away, but a sparse population enabled Nevada to be used as a place to develop weapons for national security. Nuclear testing began above ground in 1951 at the Nevada

Proving Grounds, a large area of desert and mountains about sixty-five miles northwest of Las Vegas—home to the Western Shoshone Indians, who were forced to move. It's hard to believe now, but a hundred mushroom clouds attracted tourists until 1962. Tests underground continued until 1992, and even now some tests continue. An attempt over many years by the US Department of Energy to build a nuclear waste dump in Yucca Mountain was finally put off indefinitely, in 2010, after years of protest and controversy.

In summer 2014, the first drilling for shale gas by fracking was attempted at Wells, Nevada, a few miles from Elko, and was declared "very promising." I wonder where the large amounts of water that fracking needs will come from. What will the process do to groundwater? How can we justify creating another new fossil fuel when the money could be better deployed in developing the alternatives?

Elko was the first stop on our train journeys across Nevada. Charles and Fannie noted that they had breakfast there (no complaints this time). The town was probably named by Charles Crocker, superintendent of the Central Pacific Railroad, who was fond of animal names and simply added an *o* to elk. Crofutt's guide had little to say about Elko apart from repeating a folksy anecdote about untrustworthy Indians told by Hill Beachy, who ran a stagecoach business. Complaints about the Indians were a constant refrain.

Prospectors set off from Elko and other stations in northeastern Nevada to look for gold and silver. Settlers began to arrive and to try to farm. The dryness prevented much food crop farming, even with irrigation, but it suited livestock, so farmers turned to sheep and cattle. Elko became the center of the Great Basin livestock business.

I didn't notice Elko, since my train stopped there at about 3:00 a.m. It is now the biggest city in northern Nevada, with a population of about eighteen thousand that fluctuates depending on the price of gold and its influence on the local gold mining industry, which extracts low-grade ore. When I googled "ranching elko," at the top of the results was Mona Ranch, which turns out to be a brothel; prostitution is legal in most of Nevada (but not in Las Vegas or Reno). Because so many brothels have "ranch" in their names, I had to google "Nevada cattle business" instead.

I also found that Elko is home to the National Basque Festival and the National Cowboy Poetry Gathering. I was disappointed I couldn't attend either event. Near Elko are the wild and beautiful Ruby Mountains, named for the garnets that prospectors found there. Apparently the mountains are so wild you can hike for days and never see anything except an occasional deer, antelope, elk, or mountain goat.

The City of Winnemucca (present population: seven thousand) was the next stop, 125 miles west of Elko. I was just waking up when my train stopped there. Charles and Fannie had had dinner at Battle Mountain, once a big cattle station where the train no longer stops, and didn't mention Winnemucca, which was named for a local chief of that name, also called One Moccasin. His daughter, Sarah Winnemucca, became an advocate for education and fair treatment of the Paiute and Shoshone tribes in the area.

The city is home to the First National Bank, site of a notorious bank robbery by Butch Cassidy and the Wild Bunch in September 1900. The loose group of outlaws that included Butch Cassidy and the Sundance Kid was featured in a highly popular 1969 movie. Robert Redford, the actor who played the Sundance Kid, apparently went in search of the true story of Harry Longabaugh, who seems to have gotten his nickname from being arrested for horse stealing in Sundance, Wyoming. Perhaps Redford found Donna Ernst, a woman who can trace her descent from Harry Longabaugh's brother. She wrote a biography in 2009, meticulously establishing what was fact and what was fiction in the stories.

Winnemucca is also home to the Buckaroo Hall of Fame and another annual Basque Festival. I wondered what the Basque connection was. I had an idea it might be sheepherding, and I was right. Young Basque men from rural backgrounds first came to California during the Gold Rush in the 1850s, many ending up in less-crowded Nevada. I was surprised to learn that they didn't have any experience of sheepherding back home; the work attracted them because it required no English or education and was low cost, since sheep could be managed nomadically on the free open range. A man might send back for a relative or a friend, and this began a chain migration

from a set of villages. Within fifty years, Basque owners and herders kept sheep all over the open range. Even during and after World
War II, hundreds of Basque immigrants were allowed fast-track entry
to Nevada because of a local labor shortage.

I was also curious about raising sheep as a livestock business and
why it was looked down upon as the West was settled. I discovered
that early on in the development of livestock as a business, people
were herding both sheep and cows across the West, trying to establish a living on the first-come, first-serve public grazing lands. Except
when they were being driven to market, cattle needed a land base, a
homestead ranch where cowboys could bed down, horses could be sta-
bled, and cattle could be worked, and where there was a water supply.
Sheep didn't need a land base. One herder on a horse with a dog could
work nomadically, moving a flock of one or two thousand sheep to
fresh grass every day, and camping in a tent at night. This advantage
meant that sheepherders tended to get to the grass on federal land too
quickly for the cattlemen.

The conflicts were much more prevalent in Texas, Arizona, Wyoming, and Colorado than in Nevada, so they weren't specifically about
Basques. But because sheepherding was cheaper to set up, it attracted
poorer individuals—often Mexicans or Indians in addition to Basques.
Cattlemen created a myth that sheep spoiled the grazing for cattle.
Sheepherders were called tramps, running tramp herds. Laws and
enforcement weren't in place yet, but I was shocked to discover how
violent the conflicts became and how one-sided, with thousands of
sheep slaughtered and some herders murdered.

Eating lamb is still not popular with Americans, who buy over
sixty pounds of beef for every pound of lamb. (The British, by contrast, used to eat three times more lamb than beef before cheaper beef
became available.) I thought the difference in popularity might be
related to Americans' long-standing love affair with cowboys, the cattle industry, and beef, but when I looked into it, I found that it is too
complicated for such a simplistic explanation.

Pedro and Bernardo Altube were Basque brothers who went to
California in 1850 for gold, but quickly changed to trading livestock.

Their success enabled them to buy land and more livestock, so in 1871, a few weeks before Charles and Fannie passed through Elko, they had just established the Spanish Ranch, fifty miles northwest of town. They knew it was possible to graze sheep and cattle on the same land because they eat different plants, and when the ranch was sold in 1907, it had twenty thousand head of each. It became part of the Ellison Ranching Company, which now owns 152 thousand acres of land and is one of the largest ranches in the United States. A stone bunkhouse can still be seen on their property that looks like a Basque country farmhouse.

———

I HAD LEARNED that the settlement of the West during the second half of the nineteenth century was popularized as it was happening—by books, magazines, and dime novels—and that this popularity was spread even more widely in America and Europe by Buffalo Bill's Wild West Show. I noticed that in the last part of the twentieth century, the word "myth" began to crop up in history books, suggesting a mythology of the West. Patricia Limerick described the American creation myth based on the frontier. Richard White, another revisionist historian, said that myths aren't falsehoods, but stories about history that symbolize what it means to us. Who are we and how should we act? He wrote, "The West has come to stand for independence, self-reliance, and individualism."

I couldn't work out how the settlement of the West came to stand for those particular values until I discovered a book by the British historian David Murdoch, *The American West: The Invention of a Myth* (2001), which looks at the subject from the outside, a bit like I do.

(I think an outsider can sometimes pick up things that are missed by indigenous historians, even when they fully intend to be objective. Historians still work from within their own culture, as I discovered when I was eleven. While attending school in Italy, I learned that the telephone was invented by an Italian émigré to America, Antonio Meucci, although I had previously been taught that it had been invented by an American, Alexander Graham Bell. I've never forgotten that moment of realizing that the telling of history might depend on who is telling it. More recently, after learning that inventions are usually the culmination of the work of many prior inventors, I followed up on the question of the inventor of the telephone and discovered a fascinating story. Interested readers can google "Basilio Catania.")

Murdoch suggests that the ground for the invention of the myth of the American West was laid by the popular media and then Buffalo Bill, but he goes on to claim that the myth itself was created in the early twentieth century by three individuals: Wyoming rancher and future president Teddy Roosevelt, upper-class novelist Owen Wister, and artist Frederic Remington, all well-known, highly influential easterners. Their contributions were made just after the end of the frontier, when in reality the settlement process had brought about the corporate-industrial age of large companies and wage labor. Economic growth had created wealth but not general prosperity. As self-promoters, the three men could sense the advantages of tapping into the nostalgia felt for the age of individuals settling the West. They romanticized the past and created a mythic hero for ordinary people to look up to and to emulate, extolling the values of individualism, self-reliance, and simple democracy.

In his book *Ranch Life and the Hunting Trail* (1888), Roosevelt drew on his personal experience to suggest that the cowboy was noble, courageous, and heroic. Remington presented scenes in his paintings illustrating his idea of heroism: cowboys caught in Indian fights or in a stampede, cavalry going into action. And finally, Owen Wister, fearing the West was lost, created a fictional West in his novel *The Virginian* (1902), showing a land of freedom, honesty, and integrity, where the mean and the cruel get their just deserts and the wicked perish.

Wister created the modern cowboy hero—laconic, slow to action, but invincible when aroused: "When you say that, smile!" He even invented the face-to-face street gunfight, the western ritualized duel that never existed but that followed the so-called Code of the West, an unwritten set of rules that established the requirements of living an honorable life.

In 1903, the first Western movie, *The Great Train Robbery*, was made. Its plot was inspired by a train robbery in Wyoming carried out by Butch Cassidy's gang a month before they robbed the bank in Winnemucca. Movies popularized the mythic inventions with huge success, evolving over time into many different genres, all providing magnificent escapism. The settings provided iconic scenery (with film-makers often making use of Monument Valley, Utah, with its dusty red sandstone buttes and arid expanses). Hollywood's powerful marketing ensured that Westerns spread all over the world. When I talk to British friends of my generation about writing this book and mention cow-boys and Indians, their eyes immediately light up.

Tourism took up the opportunities presented and towns across the West still promote their historic stories in myriad ways. In Tomb-stone, Arizona, actors reenact the gunfight in the reconstructed OK Corral. The city of Deadwood, South Dakota, now a National Historic Landmark, includes the saloon where Wild Bill Hickok was shot in 1876. Disneyland in Los Angeles has Frontierland, inviting visitors to do some shooting (with laser lights standing in for bullets). Even far away from the West, Disneyland in France invites visitors to Buf-falo Bill's Wild West, and Italy, home of Spaghetti Westerns, has sev-eral dude ranches that offer western-style horse riding, campfires, and roundups.

As my train continued through arid Nevada, I sat in the Obser-vation Car looking out at the vast Humboldt River Valley, wide and flat, dotted with endless gray-blue sagebrush and framed by moun-tain ranges on both sides. We passed occasional ranches, surrounded by poplar trees. The exciting stories of the Wild West provide escap-ism, but the Nevada environment presents issues that are a long way from escapist. Competition for scarce resources, especially water, con-tinues to create problems.

Las Vegas, the largest Nevada city, gets 90 percent of its water from the overused and drought-stricken Colorado River. Las Vegas water officials have been trying for years to import groundwater from across eastern Nevada to supply future growth and provide a backup supply to the Las Vegas Valley. The groundwater scheme has been opposed by rural residents, ranchers, the Western Shoshone tribe, conservationists, outdoor enthusiasts, and the Church of Jesus Christ of Latter-day Saints, which owns a cattle ranch in the area. The plans have been rejected and appealed, and in May 2015, the Supreme Court rejected yet another appeal. The problem hasn't gone away, especially with longer and longer droughts.

———

BEFORE WHITE CONTACT, the Paiutes of the Great Basin had developed a subsistence lifestyle in the harsh desert by using their knowledge and judgment to find and harvest grass seeds, pine nuts, berries, fish, small game, and waterfowl when each food source was ripe and available across a wide area. They shared the land with other native bands, each using known territories.

In the middle of finding out about the Paiutes' lifestyle, I was eerily unsettled when I visited the Discover America website (the product of a public-private marketing entity) and read this banner headline: "Nevada embraces the true spirit and the indisputable promise of the West—the freedom and sheer space to do what you want, where you want, when you want." When Nevada was dealing with its fourth year of drought, I noticed that this ode to individualism had been taken off the site.

The Paiutes have always known that Nevada, of all places, never had that freedom and sheer space. Resources were scarce and finely balanced. Any imbalance threatened survival. The moment whites came, even though the early ones just passed through, the balance was changed. Trappers exterminated the beaver, forcing the Paiute to find substitutes for the many uses they put the animal to. Livestock browsed precious grass seed crops. Miners cut down the irreplaceable pinyon trees (and their nuts) to use for their mine supports and fires.

The Paiutes were peaceful, and gratuitous killings made them flee to the mountains and hide, keeping them away from the relatively richer resources of the valley floor that they relied on. The competition for food resources finally brought out violence in them, in their aim to simply avoid starving to death. They were also forced to resort to doing wage labor in white settlements, and, if that wasn't available, begging.

There are now thirty-five federally recognized Paiute tribes in the semi-arid Great Basin region, but the Pyramid Lake Paiute Tribe, which has traditionally depended on the fish in the lake for sustenance, illustrates the enduring water-related issues that American Indians in the Great Basin have been dealing with since the 1850s.

In 1902, when a federal reclamation scheme diverted water on its way to Pyramid Lake for agricultural irrigation elsewhere, the Paiute fought against this diversion, but lost out to the agricultural interests. They kept fighting, but got nowhere. In the 1960s, an unusual ally helped their case when it was found that the decreased volume of water was endangering the rare cutthroat trout. Eventually the Paiute were supplied with fish ladders, but this still didn't stem the decline in water volume.

In 1973, an agreement was reached to increase the water coming from the Truckee, but the increase in water then brought in toxic runoff from agriculture, endangering the fish again. A 1990 agreement brought with it enough financial assistance to help the Paiute restore the fish population properly, and the lake became a mecca for keen anglers.

The Lake Pyramid Paiute may have thought their lake was safe at last, but in 2000 a private water company announced a plan to sell groundwater from a valley near Pyramid Lake to a suburb due to be developed in Reno. This dispute was finally settled in 2014 with the Paiute accepting compensation of millions of dollars and many acres of land for the water. American Indians have always needed persistence and patience.

This reminded me of another example of unusual persistence by Indians that I came across when I was looking into early contact with Indians in my home state of Vermont. Ethan Allen, one of the supposed heroes of the Vermont history I was taught, worked diligently in the 1790s to dispossess the Abenaki of their land.

I was horrified to find that the notion of the "Vanishing Race" was sometimes a cover-up for actively trying to make them vanish, even in my beloved home state. During the first half of the twentieth century, Vermont courts declared that the Abenakis didn't legally exist; a eugenics project sterilized Abenaki women; Abenaki children were sent to boarding schools to assimilate; and, in 1941, Abenakis were forced off land where they were living because it had become the Missiquoi Wildlife Refuge.

Despite all these efforts to make them vanish, the Abenaki are still there, finally getting state recognition in 2012 and still trying to get federal recognition. Some people argue that these Indians aren't really Indians, just people looking for a free ride. I suppose there are always some individuals looking for a free ride, but this shouldn't detract from the ones who have a genuine case.

Thinking about Vermont's earlier persecution of Abenakis made me realize that my own family's early internationalist outlook had a negative side. I was proud to work with Africans in Tanzania for a year after college, but it never occurred to me to find out more about American Indians in Vermont, even though an Indian family moved into a shack in our road and one of the girls joined my sixth grade class at school. It is possible I would have made friends with her if I hadn't gone to live in Italy that year, but I wonder. I suspect her poverty might have made me distance myself, despite my family's supposed openness to others, whatever their situation. I only started taking an interest in American Indians when I was discovering the reality of Indian history while repeating my great-grandparents' journey.

———

TRAVELING THROUGH the Great Basin landscape, I knew that Charles and Fannie probably didn't worry about Indian attacks on their train because of the cessation in Plains Indian hostilities at that time. I wondered, though, if they worried about train robberies, which featured in the first Western movie and many later ones. Train robberies were great for movies, but apparently didn't happen nearly as often as we might expect, and were rare when the Rices were traveling. Nevertheless, the best-known real train robbery in the West happened near Reno, Nevada, in November 1870, just a year before the Rices passed through.

A Central Pacific passenger train was overtaken by a gang of robbers who had been tipped off that the train was carrying gold worth sixty thousand dollars. They found forty-one thousand dollars in gold coins, unaware that they left behind eight thousand dollars in silver, fifteen thousand dollars in hidden gold bars, and piles of bank drafts. All of the robbers were apprehended or killed, though, before being able to enjoy their bounty. Train robbers in the movies were never so incompetent.

Stagecoaches were much more likely to be robbed, but these robberies usually occurred on the long-distance routes run by Wells Fargo & Company. Charles and Fannie used stagecoaches only for much shorter journeys, mainly in California, and they probably made sure they avoided the ones carrying money.

There was far more reason to worry about train accidents, as safety awareness developed slowly. The construction of the transcontinental railroad had been a race between two companies, building separately from the east and from the west, to see who could lay track the fastest. Safety wasn't a priority. The quality of track construction was also poor because American trains had to cover such large distances. With so little wood for fencing available, protecting the track from straying animals, which could cause accidents, was rare. A metal projecting fender, which came to be called a cowcatcher, was developed for the front of the train, but it didn't always work as intended. On one occasion, a train blew its whistle at a bull walking ahead on the track, but the bull turned and charged, derailing the train and wrecking two cars. All the bull got was a nasty headache. Railroads didn't go in for fencing until barbed wire was introduced in the late 1870s.

Even brakes weren't reliable. Trains used a primitive brake system that required a brakeman in each car to apply a hand brake at the signal of the train engineer, or sometimes just one brakeman ran from car to car. Just six weeks before Charles and Fannie started on their journey, an express train plowed into a stationary train in Revere, Massachusetts. Twenty-nine passengers died and fifty-seven were injured, including several prominent Boston citizens. Although George Westinghouse had invented and patented the much safer air brake in 1869, it took the Revere disaster to get all the railroads to install such brakes, and they weren't put on trains in the West until several years later.

Fire was an ever-present risk, too. Until the early twentieth century, train carriages were made of wood and were heated by oil or wood stoves. In the Revere accident, the express train's steam boiler burst and about a dozen people were either crushed to death by the boiler or scalded by the escaping hot water. Coal-oil lamps ignited the wreckage and burnt trapped passengers.

Before technology solved some of the safety issues, the position of the cars came to be important. Cars closest to the engine were at a greater risk of fire, smoke, and derailment than those located at the rear of the train, so luggage, mail, and emigrant cars were placed at the front to create a safety buffer for the rear cars. First-class, dining, and sleeper cars were generally located at the rear.

These risks gradually decreased as improvements were made, but the arrangement of the cars didn't change—customers had become accustomed to a configuration that demonstrated their social and economic status. There were regular news stories about the dangers and inadequacies of trains, but train travel had so much to offer that travelers were willing to take the risk.

We tend to forget that disease was a frequent killer back then too, not just accidents. When I read about women in the cattle industry, I was struck by how many spouses died, both men losing wives and women losing husbands. Being widowed was why many women took over the family cattle business. So many children died young, too. This wasn't just happening to western pioneers, either, but was prevalent everywhere.

Fannie was the eldest child in her family, born in 1844. During the following twenty-two years, her mother had ten more children, whom Fannie helped to look after. Seven of those ten children died in childhood. While all this was happening, her mother informally adopted four other motherless children. Then, when Fannie's sister Ella died in childbirth, in 1890, Fannie took in her five children, all under the age of eleven, and their father.

The autobiographical notes I have from my grandfather suggest that his mother was afraid he might inherit his father's frailties. "I can recall how carefully I was watched whenever symptoms of sore throat or cough developed, and how unconsciously I came to believe that I was destined for a short stay on this earth." Fannie probably never even told Howard about his missing aunts and uncles, not wanting to frighten him, but no wonder she worried about her own children getting ill. I always had an image of this family as comfortable, middle-class Victorians who could afford to pay for domestic help, but it must have been really tough having to deal with so many losses.

———

F ROM WINNEMUCCA, the Humboldt River and the railroad curve southwest, through more stark but beautiful wide-open landscapes, eventually reaching Reno, the last train stop in Nevada before entering California. I began musing about the early Indians' subsistence lifestyle in comparison to white Americans' faith in progress. When I was growing up in the 1950s and 1960s, I had the impression that progress, which I thought of as "life getting better," was just how things happened, and that it would continue. I was lucky to be growing up in optimistic times. Even when I spent a year volunteering in Tanzania after college and saw the extent of dire poverty, I was optimistic. I had faith in President Julius Nyerere, the charismatic first president of the newly independent country. I moved to Britain and began campaigning for social justice in the developing and the developed world.

Now I was finding out about the effects of progress in a part of my country that I had long admired. I came on this trip with my theoretical "reduce fossil fuels" campaign, and I was having to take on board the enormity of the task in real life. Progress implies constant growth. Constant growth requires making more things and using more resources. Our planet is being used up. Something has to change dramatically—much food for thought, if not for bellies.

From Reno, Charles and Fannie's train entered California through the eastern flank of the Sierra Nevada. Charles had developed a chill and was "too sick to sit up." Fannie wrote: "I was up at four a.m. to view Donner lake. The scenery was fine but much obscured by snow sheds." That Fannie got up so early to see Donner Lake shows how people were still shocked by the gruesome events that had happened there a quarter of a century earlier. When the Donner Party was trapped by heavy snow and began to starve to death, some of the party of eighty-seven resorted to cannibalism; only forty-eight survived.

Since learning about it at school, it is something I've never forgotten either.

Sitting in the Observation Lounge when we reached the mountains, I also made a point of looking out for Donner Lake. There it was, but so what? As I looked down from the train, the ugly gash of Interstate 80 cutting through the pine-covered mountains along the far side of the lake dominated the view and made it impossible for me to imagine the struggling Donner Party. If we had stopped, I could have visited the Emigrant Trail Museum near the lake and no doubt would have been mentally transported back to those times.

Our train seemed to be passing through countless tunnels and dense pine forests that closed off any possible views. In contrast, Charles and Fannie had spectacular views; most of the old-growth forest of the Sierra Nevada in those parts had then been cut down, for use in the mining industry and for building. Charles recovered enough to look out the window at Cape Horn and down "a precipice nearly one thousand feet," where the American Fork River "looked like a thread stretched through the valley below."

We emerged from the tunnels, the thick forest thinned, and we began descending from the Sierra Nevada. In the evening light, the bare soil outside the windows was terracotta-colored, with golden coppery grass standing out against the deep green of the pine trees. Down on flatter land, we stopped in Sacramento and continued directly into the setting sun and through industrialized parts of California. The train journey finished with a whimper at Emeryville's Amshack, on the east side of San Francisco Bay, where we were transferred to buses to get over the Bay Bridge into the city. It was the only time on the journey with my bike that no one offered to help me carry my things from the train to the bus, which was a surprisingly long way.

Charles and Fannie's journey's end was something of a damp squib, too. Their friend, Mr. Hanna, left them at Sacramento at noon, and soon after, they were delayed by their last car coming off the rails. The train finally stopped at Oakland, where they got a ferry to cross the seven miles of San Francisco Bay to the city. Still unwell, Charles declared, "I was glad to get to bed."

The Rices and I had arrived at San Francisco at last. I had visited the city in 1963, when I declared it the most beautiful city in America. When I first read Charles' description of San Francisco, I couldn't believe it. "San Francisco cannot be called a beautiful city. A view from any point a mile or more distant does not impress one favorably but on the contrary it looks like a dingy straggling city built upon a barren waste destitute of trees . . . as one nears the place he wonders why the streets were ever laid out over the tops of those sand hills." Did San Francisco ever really look like that? I had to find out.

# 7

# ARRIVAL IN SAN FRANCISCO

*November 5, 1871. Went to hear Dr. A. L. Stone preach
in the morning and evening, it was communion Sabbath
there. I liked him very much. Charlie some better.*

—Fannie's diary

SAN FRANCISCO was the culmination of Charles and Fannie's train
trip from Vermont, and the beginning of a six-month stay in the
city and elsewhere in California. This extended visit was more important to them than the journey across the country, but the latter was
what originally appealed to me about their trip, because of my interest in the train and the "Wild West." They arrived on a Wednesday in
the beginning of November and stayed at the upmarket Grand Hotel
on Market Street. Charles was still ill, and didn't leave their hotel
room until lunchtime on the following Sunday, after everyone else
had returned from church. The next day he and Fannie went to the
post office, where they were pleased to find four letters and a newspaper waiting for them.

I had allowed myself just over a week in San Francisco, which
wasn't nearly enough time. I looked forward to reacquainting myself
with the city that I had visited forty-five years earlier, but this time
I would look for remnants of Charles and Fannie's San Francisco.
Many changes had happened in the 137 years since their visit, including the catastrophic 1906 earthquake and fire that burned down most
of the city. I would have to work out what was still left from the city
they saw in 1871.

Their first outing, on the second day that Charles was up, was to
Cliff House, seven miles from the hotel and a must for visitors in those
days. They would have hired a horse-drawn hackney carriage and
ridden past some fine new houses and several big cemeteries before

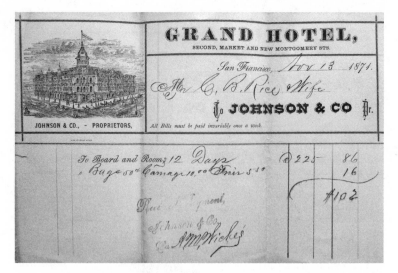

*Charles and Fannie stayed initially at the Grand Hotel
in San Francisco. They saved the hotel invoices.*

they left the protection of San Francisco Bay and rode through the Great Sand Bank, a landscape of windswept, treeless, rolling dunes overlooking the Pacific Ocean on the wilder outskirts of the city.

Cliff House was a restaurant perched on the steep, tumbled rocks looking west over the crashing surf of the Pacific. It's still there today, but the current building is its fifth incarnation. The big draw is the large colony of sea lions on the rocks just offshore. Charles and Fannie sat outside on the veranda, fascinated by watching the awkward creatures crawling up and down the rocks, yelping at and scolding each other. I imagine they also celebrated reaching the furthest western edge of the North American continent.

The next morning they caught up with writing letters to family and friends and called on new friends from the train who were staying in the same hotel. In the afternoon they went to another popular tourist attraction that has largely been forgotten. Woodward's Gardens was a combination zoo, museum, art gallery, and amusement park in a beautiful sloping setting not far from their hotel. The garden's founder, Robert Woodward, was an early entrepreneur who made his fortune during the Gold Rush by running a successful nonalcoholic hotel, the What Cheer House, and then indulged his passion for collecting plants, animals, and art at his large mansion on the dunelike hills near Mission Street. So many people came to look over the wall at his plants and animals that he finally opened his house to the public, moving his family north across San Francisco Bay to Napa. He also built the Mission Street Railway, which ran from the Ferry Building along Mission Street and ended conveniently at the front gate of his gardens (not at the Mission Dolores, which was the more logical destination).

It is hard these days to imagine how successful such a place could be, but back then it was novel for Americans to enjoy looking at the curious exotica being brought back by travelers from far-off places. Charles and Fannie were most impressed, describing almost everything they had seen. In contrast, the urbane and worldly British novelist Anthony Trollope, who stopped in San Francisco in 1875, dismissed it as "an inferior menagerie of wild beasts."

From my twenty-first-century viewpoint, I tend to agree with Trollope's comments, but knowing that Woodward's Gardens were no more, I decided I should at least check out where they had once been. It turns out the gardens have vanished so comprehensively that there isn't an iota of greenery anywhere nearby and the ground is flat. All that's left is a California Historical Site plaque on the wall of a small restaurant called Woodward Gardens, on a Mission Street corner overlooked by the noisy, raised Central Freeway. The gardens fell out of public favor when part of the Great Sand Bank (on the way to Cliff House) was made into Golden Gate Park, starting in the late 1870s.

For the park project, the city brought in enormous quantities of horse manure and water, which transformed the thousand acres of sand dunes into a soil able to support an extensive variety of grasses, flowers, shrubs, and trees. Wells were driven into an aquifer underneath and water was brought up by windmills, one of which is still there. Golden Gate Park continues to be a popular and treasured urban green oasis. Charles, who commented on the lack of good public parks, would have been impressed.

My accommodation in the city was the inexpensive but superbly situated Fisherman's Wharf Hostel, located in historic 1860s Fort

Mason. This hilltop promontory on Black Point, overlooking San Francisco Bay, had been identified early on as a good place for defensive fortifications, and in 1850 it was chosen for the site of a fort to be called Point San Jose.

During the Gold Rush, it was also identified as a fine location for building houses, and before the rule of law was established, several attractive homes were built there. At the outbreak of the Civil War, in 1861, the army reasserted control—evicting the civilian residents, whom they referred to as "genteel squatters"—and turning some of the fine homes into offices in amongst the utilitarian army barracks.

By the 1960s, the fort was no longer needed by the army and was about to be sold to the highest bidders: property developers. As it happens, the 1960s were also a time of political ferment, especially in California. People were campaigning for open spaces and parks for the carless working people of the inner cities. The Golden Gate National Recreation Area was signed into law by President Richard Nixon in 1972. It is a collection of sites with an area now over seventy-five thousand acres, on both sides of the Golden Gate Bridge. On the south side, it includes the island of Alcatraz, Fort Mason, and the Presidio, and on the north side, it includes the extensive Marin Headlands, Muir Woods, and Mount Tamalpais. To have kept such an abundance of undeveloped open spaces when cities were under so much pressure to expand was a major achievement and a lasting tribute to San Francisco, for bucking the 1960s trend of building ribbon developments in towns and cities (such as my hometown of Brattleboro).

The political activity was about more than open spaces. In 1969, a large group of American Indians from all over the country, calling themselves All Tribes, Inc., occupied the famous island of Alcatraz in San Francisco Bay. It had been a military post and then a notorious maximum-security prison from 1934 until 1963, when it was closed and the island's future left undecided. The Indians justified their seizure by subverting the early-nineteenth-century Doctrine of First Discovery that had been used to legitimize taking ownership of Indian land by European Christian countries. Tom Whitecloud wrote to his local paper, "The men at Alcatraz are simply trying to play the game you brought over. If it is not being used, stick a flag in and claim it. Move in and stay. This is, after all, the American Way."

This action, the first-ever intertribal direct action by American Indians, hit the national news headlines and raised awareness about Indian civil rights among Indian tribes and the general public. The occupation, lasting nineteen months, didn't achieve its specific demands, but it helped change federal policy regarding the American Indians and is now regarded as a key milestone in the Indians' peaceful resistance.

Other actions by Indians followed. The Wampanoag Indians, whose tribe had celebrated the first Thanksgiving 350 years earlier at Plymouth, Massachusetts, declared a Day of Mourning on Thanksgiving 1970. The American Indian Movement occupied Mount Rushmore in 1971 and the town of Wounded Knee on the Pine Ridge Reservation in 1973. American Indians had discovered the potent modern weapon of good publicity, and drew attention to their case by turning some of the iconic symbols of the American Dream on their heads, using satire and humor to catch people's attention.

Federal laws were passed in the next few years that showed new respect for Indian land rights and for the freedom of American Indians to maintain their traditional cultures, but the work isn't finished and Indian activism continues. Even a few months before I repeated my great-grandparents' train trip across America, in 2008, Indians from over a hundred tribes set off from the island of Alcatraz and walked all the way to Washington, DC, focusing on American Indian rights, environmental protection, and tackling global warming.

I had always thought of San Francisco and the rest of California as quite separate from the West of my imagination. It was beginning to sink in that this trip was bringing the two strands together, and showing me how much the city and the state were part of the story. Now that I was in California, I would learn more about western history in a broader context. It felt odd that I was learning about it this way, by repeating my great-grandparents' trip, but it also felt positive, a good way to strengthen my American roots although I live in Britain.

Indians in California were part of that saga, but their story was quite different from those of the Plains tribes. Because the California tribes had access to better natural resources than those further inland and didn't have to compete with other tribes, they sustained a subsistence lifestyle with a simple social structure of relatively small family groups. That seems to be one of the reasons they succumbed so quickly when the sophisticated Spanish came and imposed their missions on the small Indian tribes in the eighteenth century.

Gold seekers who came a hundred years later arrived with assumptions about Indians based on the powerful and often hostile Plains tribes; Californian Indians didn't stand a chance. Stories of gratuitous Indian hunting abound. Hubert Howe Bancroft, an important nineteenth-century Californian historian, wrote a history of the state in the 1880s in which he described white contact with Indians concisely. "The savages were in the way; the miners and settlers were arrogant and impatient; there were no missionaries or others still present with even the poor pretense of soul saving or civilizing. It was one of the last human hunts of civilization, and the basest and most brutal of them all." I was impressed to find such a forthright, contemporary view expressed back then. A book published in 2016, *An American Genocide: The United States and the California Indian Catastrophe, 1846-1873* by Benjamin Madley, contains detailed evidence showing that the California Indians were subjected to state-sanctioned genocide, as defined in the UN Genocide Convention of 1948.

After the reversal of the 1940s federal policy of terminating tribes (informally, in the late 1960s, and officially, in 1988), a process was devised for tribes to be recognized as valid, and there are 567 federally recognized tribes in today's United States. Indians have learned how to use the American legal system, but the legal system relevant to Indians is riddled with problems. It isn't easy to gain recognition because of the requirement for written evidence, and it is particularly difficult for Indians from the plethora of small tribes in California, because they were so persecuted that they often pretended to be American or Mexican. Very little evidence of their Indian antecedents exists. The process is also expensive, requiring a team of anthropologists, historians, lawyers, and sometimes professional lobbyists to gather data to clear the Bureau of Indian Affair's legal hurdles. The

BIA is understaffed and there are still two hundred groups waiting for a result on their application for recognition. One tribe waited thirty-two years.

From the terrace of my Fisherman's Wharf Hostel, I looked out across San Francisco Bay to Alcatraz, now a National Park attracting crowds of tourists who learn about its role in Indian history as well as its time as an infamous penitentiary. This view from the hostel is probably better than the view from any hotel in the city, looking out to the Golden Gate Bridge as well as to Alcatraz. The sun sinking into the Pacific Ocean behind the dark outline of the bridge regularly paints the skies fiery colors, reflected gloriously in the bay's waters. Charles and Fannie no doubt saw some gorgeous sunsets, too, but their hotel faced the other way, toward the barren hilltops that Charles had described as ugly.

Perhaps Charles' curiosity about the bare tops is what drew him to climb by himself up Telegraph Hill. He didn't comment on his original opinion of the city view, but he said without reservation that the views and landscapes all around were marvelous—the army fortifications below (now housing my hostel), the mountains across the bay to the north, the bay islands, and the small towns to the east of the bay: Oakland, Brooklyn, and Alameda. Not having a camera, he described everything in much more detail than I have given, even listing all the streets he could identify,

I decided it would be fun to go on the free walking tour offered by my hostel. Our guide was Henry, native of New Jersey, who provided an entertaining narrative and an excellent overview of the city. He took us to the top of Russian Hill, where we could look down vertiginous Lombard Street with its amazing corkscrew bends. We stopped at the Cable Car Museum and I learned that the cable car, such a popular attraction on San Francisco's steep hills, was nearly abolished in 1947.

Elected on a pledge of efficient government, the mayor at that time said cable cars were obsolete and should be taken out. Fortunately, leaders of women's civic groups in San Francisco mounted a successful campaign in opposition, making the case that any financial loss to the city as a result of the cable cars could be regained by

*Here I am in San Francisco.*

promoting them to visitors—who have been flocking to the city from all over the world ever since. Hallelujah! I'm just sorry that Charles and Fannie missed riding one. I boarded one of the cars again and remembered with fondness my exhilarating first ride in 1963.

The Cable Car Museum is near Chinatown, where Henry took us to the Golden Gate Fortune Cookie Factory, and we crowded in to see a Chinese woman making fortune cookies by hand. She gave one free to each of us and then charged us for taking photos. After Henry left us in Chinatown, I continued to wander around to get a sense of the area. Chinatown became a focal point for Charles and Fannie, but not until the Chinese New Year, three months after their arrival.

My hair was getting shaggier and shaggier, so I went into the Happy Hair Studio, one of many Chinese hairdressers. Only one hairdresser was on duty, who apparently spoke no English (though he probably understood it), and he proceeded to do exactly what I wanted, charging me just nine dollars (plus my tip). I wondered how he survived charging such prices, and guessed it might be because of the Chinese penchant for doing things collectively and supporting each other.

CHARLES AND FANNIE'S life developed a routine in the several weeks before they set off for a six-week trip to southern California. Their busy days included calling on a surprising number of friends new and old, going to the post office and the library (with separate reading rooms for Gentlemen and Ladies), receiving and writing a constant stream of letters, remarking on the San Francisco fog, going on outings to tourist sites around the city, and attending church services, prayer meetings, and Sunday School. On November 17, Charles wrote, "We have no excitement but live very quietly, which is as we wish it to be." It would have been too tame for me, but I think they were probably relieved to have reached civilization again so they could relax and just enjoy day-to-day life, even though they also had the same urge I have to explore and learn about new places and people.

Both Charles and Fannie mentioned books they were reading. They also held group readings with friends, which took place in their hotel. Several times Charles read out loud from the book *Robert Falconer* (1868), which I've found in Project Gutenberg, the free online library of old books. By George MacDonald, it tells the story of a Scottish boy living with his strict Calvinist grandmother, trying to find his absent father and to be a good Christian. It is semi-autobiographical and reflects the author's own search for a less Calvinist Christianity and a more loving God.

Charles also recorded reading Dickens, *David Copperfield* and *Great Expectations*, but the rest of his and Fannie's books strike me as sanctimonious drivel. (Of course, I would probably have been pleased enough if it were Wild West drivel.) One of Charles' books was *Mrs. Jerningham's Journal* (1869) by Fanny Wheeler Hart, which I found online. It's a short book in verse about a newly married young woman who starts off unhappy but by the end has fallen in love with her husband. My feminist principles made me bristle at the Victorians' blatant sexism, but I told myself not to judge too harshly. It was a "product of its time."

I was puzzled at Fannie's list of books until it occurred to me that she may have been reading books she could recommend to her Sunday

School class, with whom she was corresponding. One book on the list was *Snail-shell Harbor* (1870) by J. H. Langille, part of a collection published by Henry Hoyt of Boston. Hoyt specialized in books described as "eminently evangelical in character and spirit . . . no safer or better works for the Sunday school or family are known to the Christian public than the issues of this house." A quick look at *Snail-shell Harbor* indicates that it was about new immigrants trying to make a living by fishing on Lake Michigan, but lacking the support of a church or pastor. By the end of the book they have a pastor, a church, and a much more godly life. It wasn't a typical Wild West dime novel, but its preoccupations were probably common themes of frontier life that haven't persisted in the myths of more recent times. The struggle to bring religion to the West was certainly a frequent ingredient of Charles and Fannie's observations.

It was when they were in San Francisco that the amount of time they devoted to religion really hit me. Church on Sunday wasn't just a service in the morning. They went to Sunday School in the afternoon and to another church service, usually at a different church, in the evening. (Harry Jones, a parson from London, described going to six church services in San Francisco one Sunday, so the Rices weren't the only ones undertaking religious tourism.) They also attended evening prayer meetings at various venues in the middle of the week, including the Pavilion Skating Rink. The church they attended most often was their own denomination's First Congregational Church, but they also went to Presbyterian, Episcopal, Methodist, and Unitarian services.

A typical Sunday in San Francisco, recorded by Charles, went thus: "Sunday Feby 18th: Rainy all the forenoon. Beautiful and pleasant in afternoon. Attended service at Howard Presbyterian in the morning. Singing splendid. Dr. Carpenter preached. Dr. Stone preached at the Skating Rink in the evening. Subject second coming of Christ. Audience about 1,500." One thousand, five hundred people at a San Francisco religious gathering—my jaw dropped when I read that!

Even more surprising is that the services they attended weren't always Christian. One Saturday they attended a service at the Jewish Synagogue, where "the music was charming." I was intrigued that they had gone to a Jewish ceremony. Unitarians' belief that Jesus was a great prophet, but not divine, means that we emphasize our Judeo-Christian heritage, so I've always felt a connection with Judaism—but as far as I knew, Congregationalists don't. The synagogue they went to must have been the Congregation Sherith Israel, which had just built a synagogue on the corner of Post and Taylor Streets. A second synagogue, two miles west on Lake Street, had been founded by Congregation Emanu-El in 1850. Two synagogues suggest a good-sized Jewish community.

With the rampant racism shown to the Chinese, the Mexicans, and the Indians, I assumed that anti-Semitism was also common, but apparently it was surprisingly rare. Because Jewish San Franciscans were predominantly from Germany, and German culture was held in high esteem in the United States, they were not seen as intruders or outsiders. On the contrary, Jews were central to the formation of a cosmopolitan San Francisco. Their cultural background raised their reputation in communities that valued cultural activity, and they also had much-needed commercial skills that were less common in other immigrant groups. Merchants were essential in the unstructured towns and cities of the expanding country if local economies were to flourish.

Charles and Fannie would no doubt have felt comfortable in Jewish company. It's a shame they didn't meet Levi Strauss, a prominent member of the other Jewish synagogue. He was on the verge of producing the sturdy work overalls made out of cloth imported from Nimes, France, that famously became known as blue jeans (or Levis). The cloth came to be called denim (from "de Nimes"). They made him a fortune.

I knew from a past diary entry that Charles had not been tolerant of Catholicism when he was younger. While at a Civil War Parole Camp in 1862, he wrote that he had attended the Catholic Service and was "perfectly disgusted with their proceedings." His feelings were probably fueled by the long antagonism between Catholic and Protestant Christians after the Reformation. In San Francisco, he and Fannie visited the Catholic Dolores Mission, established by the Spanish in 1776, and he noted that all the scenes represented suffering and that the Catholic priests seemed to want to scare the first Indians into accepting the Christian religion.

Although religion was a constant refrain, Charles and Fannie rarely described the food they ate. Fannie recorded eating oysters in Santa Barbara, which made me wonder what else they dined on, so I unearthed other visitors' observations of eating in California. Harry Jones, a London parson, was struck by the "excellent and abundant fruit and wine. Strawberries are grown the whole year round; and grapes, figs, pears, melons, limes and peaches might make the mouth of a statue water. . . . Venison, and occasionally turtle, salmon, smelts, perch, cod, oysters, frogs, squirrels, quails, turkeys, beef, mutton, pork etc., with pastry and ice creams." I was tickled by his description of eating an ear of corn: "Indian corn, of which the green ear is boiled whole, buttered and eaten as a dog gnaws a bone."

It was time to look for more of what remained of Charles and Fannie's 1870s San Francisco. Just below my hostel, bike paths run along the bay's waterfront, to the west toward the Golden Gate Bridge and to the east past piers lining the Embarcadero and the older part of the city. I set off eastward. On the way, I stopped on Market Street at the foot of the California Street cable car and was surprised to find myself looking, by chance, at a simple monument in black polished granite to my favorite poet, New Englander Robert Frost.

Frost is my favorite poet partly because my father, who once aspired to be a poet, knew and admired him. They met when Dad was on the Vermont Board of Education and Frost lived in Vermont. In 1932, Dad wrote a book about how poetry should be part of the school curriculum, suggesting several of Frost's poems that could be used as examples of New England regionalism. He wrote, "Frost could be none other than a New Englander." He felt a kinship with Frost and admired his affinity for rural people and landscapes. He gave me books of Frost's poems for my birthdays, with images and characters with which I was already familiar, so my strong sense of place regarding the area where I grew up was further enriched by Frost's poetry.

I had no idea, until I saw the granite memorial, that Frost was born in San Francisco, not New England, just two years after Charles and Fannie visited. His family lived in seven different houses there until his violent and unstable father, city editor of the *Daily Evening*

*Post,* died of tuberculosis in 1885 (the same year that Charles also died of TB).

I was particularly taken aback by coming across Frost in this way because I had come across him equally unexpectedly in England, the previous summer, when I had visited an exhibition in Gloucestershire on the Dymock Poets. In the years leading up to the World War I, several English poets, including Rupert Brooke and Edward Thomas, were joined in Dymock by Robert Frost and his family. There Frost enjoyed some fruitful years in the company of like-minded writers and successfully launched his career as a poet.

One of Robert Frost's poems, *A Peck of Gold,* refers to his time in San Francisco:

*Dust always blowing about the town,*
*Except when sea-fog laid it down,*
*And I was one of the children told*
*Some of the blowing dust was gold.*

*All the dust the wind blew high*
*Appeared like gold in the sunset sky,*
*But I was one of the children told*
*Some of the dust was really gold.*

*Such was life in the Golden Gate:*
*Gold dusted all we drank and ate,*
*And I was one of the children told,*
*We all must eat our peck of gold.*

Frost wrote *A Peck of Gold* in 1928, about his memories of San Francisco from about 1880. I think he is describing his sense of the place then. He evokes children's gullibility and confusion about being told the prevailing clouds of dust in the city contained gold. He highlights the contrast between rags and riches, and the elusive hopes of transforming one to the other.

So now, in San Francisco, I learned that Frost was a seasoned traveler, rather like my great-grandparents and me. Nevertheless, he did put down roots and become a New Englander—developing a sense of place doesn't require being born there. It made me understand that, on this trip, I was looking at the West as a place in history and finding that my own childhood sense of that place was at odds with what my great-grandparents described. Maybe exploring the concept of sense of place could clarify some things.

There isn't one accepted definition of a sense of place, but I prefer the one that implies an interaction between humans and an environment, an interaction that evolves because people and places change over time and influence each other. My great-grandparents' diaries had shown me that my childhood perceptions, based on a mid-twentieth-century interpretation of the settling of the West, were out of step with their interpretation, during a time when settlement was still in full flow, but also out of step with what I was learning in the present day. As with regard to the value and role of trees in Nebraska, we live and learn.

Charles and Fannie were enthralled by the positive effects of progress. I learned, 137 years later, that the settling of the West had not been as romantic as my childhood memories suggested, and I was noticing the high costs of progress. But I can understand Charles and Fannie's views being of their time, and I just feel grateful to their memory for prompting me to undertake this journey and broaden my own knowledge and understanding.

From Robert Frost's memorial on Market Street, I resumed my search for Charles and Fannie's San Francisco, leaving the center of town and cycling east through streets that were rather rundown and scruffy. I soon passed two Gold Rush–era frame houses with white picket fences that must have been there in 1871—one now providing accommodation for people with HIV/AIDS, and the other a shelter for people in recovery from drug and alcohol addiction.

I knew that several of the local residents that Charles and Fannie had visited lived in a fashionable area southeast of Market Street called Rincon Hill, and I had looked at some old photos of the beautiful residences and gardens there. It had subsequently fallen on hard times even before the earthquake, but I wanted to see what it looked like now. I was surprised to discover that, like Woodward Gardens, it had completely disappeared. Not only were the houses gone, but the hill had been flattened, and the area was dominated by the raised Interstate 80 on its way to the Bay Bridge. All I found was a small plaque marking it as a Historic Landmark, attached to an old office building that actually had a highway access road wrapped around it. Rincon Hill was clearly in the wrong place back then. Commerce gained the upper hand when the hill was split in two in 1869 in order to flatten Second Street, which led to land designated for factories. Residents fought the project, but commercial interests prevailed. In 1870, the visiting London parson that I mentioned earlier, the one who described the food, came looking for the bishop of California at 348 Second Street and discovered a "fresh-made cliff... and a crowd of navvies carting away stuff." He was told that the bishop's house had "tumbled down into the street," and that the bishop was living on the other side of the city. When Charles and Fannie visited, Rincon still had good houses built by merchants and sea captains, but it went downhill soon after. The name is all that lives on, here and there, including in OneRincon, a colossal high-rise apartment block built recently. It was sobering to realize how urban areas can change so much over relatively short periods.

Since I was in an old part of San Francisco that wasn't an obvious tourist attraction, I chose to explore some more. On the map, I spotted another crooked street that attracted me because it was named Vermont Street, same as my home state. It had seven turns instead of eight, but its gradient going up Portrero Hill was even steeper than that of Lombard Street and it promised some good views. I gained the top from a gentler direction and found a spot where I could look north and admire the skyscrapers rising from the Financial District. Turning to face southwest, I found a stunning view of the Twin Peaks that Charles had climbed.

I thought this was the hinterlands when Charles and Fannie were here, but when I checked, I discovered that at that time it had already undergone the typically frenzied changes so common in those days for the sake of progress. Portrero Hill is just a puny reminder of a substantial ridge of hard serpentine rock that jutted out into the Bay. Most of it was blasted away to flatten the shoreline for industry and shipping and to provide rock for filling in the marshy cove called Mission Bay.

Cycling down the hairpin turns was good fun, but the Bayshore Freeway at the bottom rather spoiled the effect. Heading back to the hostel, I spotted two more pre-1871 houses in Guerrero Street that led me into a colorful South Asian and Latino area, full of vibrant restaurants and cafes. I later identified it as the Mission District, which I was then told was characterized by an unusual combination of gang warfare and gentrification, so beware. I had cycled serenely along the streets unaware of any possible trouble.

I was disappointed that my search for 1871 San Francisco wasn't a success, having found just a few old houses here and there. Too much was changed by the 1906 earthquake and the major human interventions before and after. Maybe I just had to accept that change was an inevitable factor. Then I remembered an important development early in the city's inception that had not changed: the 1830s street plan that advocated plonking a square street grid onto the hills. In 1839, while still part of Mexico, the town had created a small grid plan to make sellable lots around what is now Portsmouth Square, an area that wasn't unduly hilly. In 1847, after Americans had taken charge, an Irish engineer expanded the grid, but wanted to make terraced roads to provide an easier gradient for getting up the prominent hills, like Nob Hill and Russian Hill. Residents supported him, but the property owners wanted easy-to-sell square blocks of land, and got their way.

When Charles declared in 1871 that the straggly city was built on a barren wasteland, the street grid still reflected the short-sighted plans of the early property owners, who wanted the ease and efficiency of straight boundaries. They hadn't taken into account the obvious flaw, that horses couldn't pull a wagon up such gradients. So the steep land remained undeveloped.

Another interesting discovery I made at the Cable Car Museum was that the cable car finally solved the problem. Two years after Charles and Fannie visited the city, the world's first cable-operated electric street car was installed, finally making the steepest hills accessible. The building of the quirky, Victorian row houses—the iconic Painted Ladies, as they are known—began in earnest. But the street grid still provided the original bones of Charles and Fannie's San Francisco, so I continued to explore.

The hills-be-damned street plan certainly made cycling in San Francisco an adventure. The steepest hills weren't impossible for me to cycle up, but I tried to avoid them if I could. I found myself devising complicated zigzag routes for getting from A to B. My bike map tried to help by coloring the streets according to the steepness of the gradient, but as a visitor unfamiliar with the city, I couldn't always know, as I approached, the essential fact of whether the gradient was up or down.

Some streets had cycle lanes, so I headed for those. I was cycling in a dedicated lane, looking for the Caltrain station, when I came across a section with portable signs saying "No Parking/Tow Away Zone." Right in the middle of them, a parked car was blocking the cycle lane, which really ticked me off. I stopped, picked up one of the signs, and placed it on the front of the car—which set off the car alarm, so I skedaddled.

Continuing my explorations, I found myself on Pacific Avenue, which has some particularly grand late-nineteenth-century houses, all different. Then I headed down Steiner Street, turned left on Post Street, and was pleased to find myself, quite unexpectedly, in Japan Town.

Before they left San Francisco, Charles and Fannie bought "a three corner box at the Japanese Bazaar for $4.00," so I was gratified that I had found a bit of their city. I have since learned that there was no Japan Town in 1871, and the Japanese Bazaar was run by someone who wasn't Japanese, probably in Chinatown. The area that is now Japan Town was still sandy and bare when Charles and Fannie were there.

Apparently, Japan Town is popular with visiting Japanese today because they can buy things that are no longer available at home, such as the homemade soybean sweets called *manju*, served at celebrations. Apart from the unfortunate years during World War II when long-established Japanese Americans were interned in case they were spies, *manju* have been made by the Okimara family since 1906—but they say no one is making them in Japan any longer.

I left Japan Town to return to the hostel and got lost, so I stopped to consult my map. I noticed that someone was shouting at me from across the street, and I looked over to see a man in a dark suit and tie with a briefcase striding towards me. What could he want, I wondered? Then I heard what he was saying: "I've got a Bike Friday, too. Great bikes! Where are you going on yours? Do you need some help finding it?" Bike Friday enthusiasts are all over America, and they make a point of acknowledging each other and talking about the bikes whenever possible. He wasn't the first person to approach me, nor the last, but in his business suit, I didn't exactly associate him with cycling. We chatted amiably for a while about traveling on Bike Fridays and then continued on our separate ways.

I had to admit that Charles and Fannie's activities were too urban Victorian for my taste—rather dull, and very far from my image of the Wild West. I wondered what else was happening around San Francisco while they were dropping off their calling cards, attending church, and visiting gardens, zoos, and the seaside.

I learned that it wasn't nearly as civilized as their diaries implied. Its rapid early growth during the 1849 Gold Rush free-for-all had created a Wild West town that lacked only the cowboys. Then the 1859 silver boom in Nevada had brought another influx of money to the city, making it the third most important American sea trade center after New York and Boston.

By 1871, however, San Francisco had only one police officer for every 1,445 inhabitants, compared to New York City, with one for every 464 inhabitants, and London, with one for every 303. Policemen in San Francisco always patrolled in pairs. There was one murder a week, on average. Like Omaha, the city had a growing number of residents who were trying to build a law-abiding, urban economy and culture with some success, but a rough and lawless underbelly was still a major problem.

In the library, I found a vivid account written by a Mexican, Guillermo Prieto, called *San Francisco in the Seventies: The City as Viewed by a Mexican Political Exile* (1877). He described Dupont Street (now Grant Avenue) as the red light district, with "sirens who devote their charms to luring the fragile, and display themselves at their windows . . . At night a group of beauties in fancy dress crowd the doorways. Sultanas, priestesses, Grecian women, Amazons, Olympian goddesses call out in every language for the traveler to rest his weariness and exalt the virtues of their various establishments . . . They dispose of their attractions as a piece of merchandise. The traffic is in cold blood, as if it were a question of liquors or cloth."

The area was known as the Barbary Coast, a name borrowed from the Barbary Coast of North Africa, which apparently was known for the same kind of predatory dives. Albert Evans, a reporter on the *Alta California* newspaper at the time, described it as "the haunt of the low and the vile of every kind. The petty thief, the house burglar, the tramp, the whore monger, lewd women, cut-throats, murderers, are all found here . . . Licentiousness, debauchery, pollution, loathsome disease, insanity from dissipation, misery, poverty, wealth, profanity, blasphemy, and death, are here. And Hell, yawning to receive the putrid mass, is here also." I marvel at the extravagance of Victorian prose.

What did Charles and Fannie make of it? They wrote not a word about it in their diaries. Guillermo Prieto pointed out that the aspect of the city changed at night. Most of Charles and Fannie's evenings were spent in their hotel, several blocks away, reading their books with Christian moral themes, and if they went out in the evening, they would have been driven from door to door. Still, they must have known what was going on. But perhaps it was like the bad things that assail us in the newspapers and television today—we live our lives largely as if those things are not happening.

Some visitors to the city were bolder. In 1877, Miriam Leslie, a New York magazine editor, wrote about her visit to an opium den in her book *California: A Pleasure Trip from Gotham City to the Golden Gate* (1877). She made an observation about the Chinese man who had talked to them while he was still lucid, just beginning his first pipe. "We bade him good-by and went out, his eyes following us with a look and a laugh strangely resembling a sneer. Perhaps . . . there is something about the first stages of opium intoxication dispelling to customary caution and disguise, for in that sneering look and laugh we seemed at last to get the true expression of feeling which forever haunts the writer as the real meaning underlying the bland, smiling or inane exterior, presented to us by these Celestials."

I know Charles walked near this rough area because he described the unorthodox way that land in the bay had been reclaimed. The streets of Davis, Front, Battery, and Sansome, and a part of Montgomery Street, were originally part of the bay, and ships used to come up as far as Sansome Street. Charles described seeing an old rickety building, bearing the sign "Niantic Hotel," at the corner of Sansome and Clay, built upon the hulk of the old store ship, Niantic. After carrying 248 gold-seekers from Panama to San Francisco Bay in the summer of 1849, the Niantic was beached and the whole crew abandoned it to join the gold-seekers. It was made into a hotel, and the area belowdecks was converted to warehouses entered by doorways on the sides. A fire in 1851 destroyed all but the submerged hulk, which was then used as the foundation for a new Niantic Hotel, a famous hostelry that lasted until 1872.

A number of other ships were deserted by their crews during the Gold Rush, their remains helping to reclaim the land from the harbor. Since the land was reclaimed, creating foundations for new buildings regularly brings up relics from these old ships. As late as 2005, the *Candace*, built in Boston in 1818, was discovered twenty feet below Folsom Street.

Meanwhile, Charles ascertained that the steamer *California* sailed to Santa Barbara, and bought them two tickets for twelve dollars each, including board. After six weeks in San Francisco, they were about to leave for their excursion south to Santa Barbara and Los Angeles.

# 8

# AN EXCURSION TO SANTA BARBARA AND LOS ANGELES

*December 13, 1871. Had letters from*
*Missy Clark, Helen and Mrs. H. Charlie one from*
*Rev Dickson. Started on the Steamship "California" for*
*Santa B. I kept my Berth all day from sea sickness.*
—Fannie's diary

WHEN RECORDING this journey in his diary, Charles poked fun at the steamship lines, writing that they were on to a money-making scheme because of all the passengers who had paid for meals they couldn't eat because of seasickness. Not having seasickness, he could mock—it was Fannie who suffered.

At Santa Barbara, the lack of a wharf meant the steamer had to anchor a mile off the coast and passengers had to disembark via a small boat that pitched about wildly. Fannie described it: "Arrived about six, a boat came for us. I *did not* enjoy the landing." A full-sized wharf was built the following year, making the arrival of steamers less traumatic and opening the way for a growing number of tourists. Charles and Fannie were definitely pioneer tourists on this trip.

When I looked at using my Amtrak rail pass to get from San Francisco to Santa Barbara, I worked out that I would have to retrace my steps and return to the eastern side of the bay to get to Amtrak's north-south inland route. Alternatively, Caltrain's commuter service could take me directly south down the San Francisco peninsula, through high-tech Silicon Valley, to join Amtrak in San Jose.

I went by Caltrain, and was amazed at the startling contrast with old-fashioned, lumbering Amtrak. Many young, well-off, environmentally aware professionals living in San Francisco and Silicon Valley commute to work by train, using their bikes at each end. When I got on the Caltrain Bike Car, I couldn't believe my eyes. I was used to British trains that were under acute pressure to take more passengers, so space for bicycles has diminished depressingly. The Caltrain Bike Car was purpose-built for thirty-two cyclists and thirty-two bikes, with a smart design for getting lots of cyclists on and off at stations remarkably efficiently. Filled with envy, I discussed the vagaries of bikes and train travel with a local bicycle commuter who was also curious about my trip.

Our conversation moved on to climate change, and he told me how proud he was that the state of California, which has an economy the size of France, passed a landmark law in 2006 that called for the state to reduce carbon pollution to 1990 levels by 2020. California continues to lead on environmental issues, and I am impressed and heartened by the state's progressive policies. I wish Britain were not so centralized, which substantially limits what local governments in the U.K. can do.

When I got to San Jose, the Amtrak train was three and a half hours late, reminding me, with a sinking heart, of Amtrak's serious punctuality problems. And when I finally arrived in Santa Barbara, I found, to my intense irritation, that Amtrak had forgotten to take my checked-in bike off the train. I had to complete a form, and was told I'd be called as soon as it was back in Santa Barbara. Fortunately, I had agreed to my hosts' offer to meet me at the station with their car.

As soon as Charles and Fannie arrived in Santa Barbara, they sounded like they were on vacation for the first time since they had left home. They stayed at Lincoln House, opened the previous year by Boston banker Amasa Lincoln (a cousin of Abraham Lincoln). It was built to look like a New England–style boarding house, using wood that had been imported from Oregon, and it is still there, now renamed the Upham Hotel and billed as "the oldest continuously operating hostelry in Southern California," Maybe the small coastal town and the hotel reminded the Rices of past vacations on Cape Cod, overlooking the Atlantic Ocean, which they had recorded in their diaries.

Their days were taken up by walks to the beach, horseback rides, and games at the hotel. On the first day of their stay, Fannie sat on the "piazza" while Charles went rabbit hunting with other hotel guests.

By the second day, Fannie had fully recovered from her seasickness. "Charlie and I took a horseback ride some three miles up the valley, had lots of fun with our horses."

Using horses for transport was still taken for granted back then. At home they were fond of their horse, Hero, who pulled their buggy around locally. On this trip, unless they were in a city, they usually went on horseback for a day out. I expect they used horses for local transport the way I use a bicycle. Fannie no doubt rode sidesaddle, as was the custom for women.

The weather was much milder than in New England, with a mixture of sun, showers, and rain. In the following days, Charles and some men went off on horseback, hunting for small game and bagging some ground squirrels (similar to prairie dogs, but smaller). Fannie went to the beach with other guests or stayed in the hotel and sewed on her "ginghams." (She sewed on her "worsteds" in San Francisco. Hand-sewing seemed to be a Victorian lady's regular chore, even on holiday.) Their visit sounded more relaxed than their stay in San Francisco.

My ATC hosts in Santa Barbara were quite different from Ruth and Larry in Omaha and Mary in Salt Lake City. Robert was a retired real estate lawyer and Deby, from Indonesia, was much younger. They were vegetarians and teetotalers, went to bed at sunset, and rose at dawn. They also had a McCain and Palin presidential election sign in the front yard. I thought about mentioning my support for Obama, but decided to avoid talking politics. I rationalized this on the basis that Robert's law background meant he would run rings around me in any debate or argument. At least we had cycling in common, as they had gone on several long cycling tours in European countries in the past, though they cycled rarely now. They turned out to be especially caring hosts.

That night I slept badly, not knowing when I would get my bike back. I didn't trust Amtrak to call me, so straight after breakfast I caught a bus into town. Local buses are great fun. Everyone knows everyone else and the banter resonates. The gregarious woman across the aisle quizzed me on what I was doing in Santa Barbara. The bus driver shouted at a passenger, "Sit down and wait until the bus stops!"

When it stopped, she got up from her seat and helped another passenger to assemble his wheeled walker. Everyone told me when it was my stop for Amtrak, and wished me well.

I walked into the station and immediately spotted the black bag with my bike, my precious Bike Friday. I was so relieved I burst into tears. I hadn't realized that I had gotten so attached to it! I eagerly reassembled the bike and set off to have a look at Santa Barbara, first noticing that the Amtrak station here is not an Amshack, but was built in the Spanish Mission Revival Style in 1902 and restored in 2000. I picked up a leaflet about historic places and meandered around on my bike in the oldest part of town, looking at the architecture and enjoying the sunshine and people-watching.

First stop was the site of the Spanish Presidio founded in 1782, now a State Historic Park. Looking at the long, low adobe buildings from the corner of East Canon Perdido Street and Santa Barbara Street, I could imagine the rectangular shape of the original structure. (I understand a lot more reconstruction has been done since my visit.) At last, I was touching base with my country's eye-catching Spanish history. I was in El Pueblo Viejo, the Old Town, amid the Spanish-themed adobe buildings with white stucco walls and terracotta-tiled roofs, set off by the vivid blue skies. Around the corner, I cycled past La Casa de la Guerra, which has an open courtyard with low covered verandas facing the street on three sides, and I resolved to come back.

I explored the smart shopping area on nearby State Street and then went to find the hotel where Charles and Fannie stayed, not far away. This took me into an old residential area with a more conventional American feel, with nineteenth- and twentieth-century houses. Soon I reached Upham House, and, apart from the palm trees, I was immediately transported back to New England. The house was clad in traditional New England wooden clapboards, and a deep welcoming porch was attached to the front, continuing on both sides. It must have made Charles and Fannie feel at home, a feeling they valued—the opposite of my buzz at being immersed in the foreign Spanish look.

I did some more meandering, looking for original adobe houses built before the Americans arrived, but they are not always easy to find, with several hidden away behind greenery. Eventually, it was time to return to my ATC hosts, whose house was three miles north on the outskirts of town. On my way, I made a detour to pass by the Old Mission, which sits on a high piece of land looking out over the town to the ocean. I liked Santa Barbara.

Back in 1871, it was December, and Christmas was approaching for the guests at Lincoln House. On Christmas Day, Charles recorded that it was foggy but not rainy; they took a ride on horseback in the afternoon, and had a molasses candy pull in the evening. Fannie wrote, "Of all the stupid Christmases, this is the most so. Wrote to Mrs. Howard as normal. Had a candy pull in the evening and enjoyed it much." Stupid Christmas? Did she mean that the summery weather of Santa Barbara was stupid at Christmas, compared to that of wintry Vermont? Or did stupid mean something else?

I looked through my transcript of their diaries again. Their entries over the years marked a slow change to what Christmas meant to them. The Congregationalist Church, because of its Pilgrim roots, still deemed Christmas not worth celebrating because nothing in the Bible justified it, but Congregationalists were slowly being influenced by other churchs' beliefs and customs. For the Christmas of 1868, Fannie mentioned exchanging presents for the first time. In 1870, the government declared Christmas a public holiday, part of the post–Civil War policy of creating a national culture with national holidays. But after that Christmas in Santa Barbara, the Rices mentioned nothing other than exchanging presents until the 1880s. Perhaps Fannie was put out by other guests at their hotel being more celebratory than she thought proper. Since she clearly enjoyed the candy pull in the evening, I assume candy-pulling didn't count as celebrating Christmas.

The next day I visited the Santa Barbara Library, which is in a lovely Spanish Colonial Revival–style building, and found out more about Santa Barbara, starting with the Chumash Indians who had lived there. The Chumash created rock art, now preserved in the Chumash Painted Cave Historic Park, eleven miles northwest of town. I wished I could fit it in to my visit, but I didn't have enough time. I longed to linger in California for seven months, like my great-grandparents.

Buying food for a picnic, I found my way to the waterfront to see

*Santa Barbara homeless people collecting recyclable items for cash.*

the beach where Charles and Fannie came ashore in wild conditions, and then continued along a cycle path to a good spot by the ocean to have lunch. Nearby, next to some well-appointed public restrooms, the local homeless community was gathered. It occurred to me that Santa Barbara's clement climate must be an attraction for homeless people. Many had bicycles loaded high with bags of recyclable material that would get them a cash payment. One had decorated his bike and his hair with dozens of rainbow-colored ribbons. Because I had bought my bike for carrying my belongings on a long journey across America, I had chosen the name "Bag Lady Cyclist" for the customized name label Bike Friday put on my cross bar. I was likening myself to the cyclists I had noticed (probably homeless) who had all their belongings with them in bags. Suddenly I felt like an imposter.

I bought food for my dinner in a swanky supermarket called Ralph's and cycled back to Robert and Deby's house. Only when I got off my bike did I discover that my briefcase, with my journal and all my notes—all irreplaceable—had fallen off, though they had been secured with a bungee. I was distraught, and rushed to tell Robert and Deby. They wouldn't let me cycle back into town, but insisted on searching for the briefcase by car. I had cycled past the Greyhound bus station, so if it had fallen off there, my chances of getting it back were low. We went to the Greyhound station, then other garages and businesses, asking if my briefcase had been handed in. Nothing, no luck. Robert called the police but was told we would have to try again the next day when Lost and Found was open. I was in despair.

Later in the evening, Deby answered a knock at their door and opened it to find a woman holding my briefcase! She had picked it up in State Street and taken it home, where she had looked at the contents and understood what it must mean to the owner. She then found my itinerary with the address of my ATC hosts and came to give it back to me. I thanked her again and again, and told her I was blessed and she was an angel, language I'm not in the habit of using. It was a catastrophe averted, and I thanked my lucky stars, glad that my carelessness was mitigated somewhat by my efficiency in printing out an itinerary with my contact details.

———

SOON AFTER THEY ARRIVED in Santa Barbara, Charles and Fannie rode on horseback with another hotel guest to a hot spring about six miles from town. Charles noted that his bath there was ninety-eight degrees. The day before, Fannie had written a puzzling comment: "Charlie was weighed, still improves." Had his illness on the train journey lingered on while they were in San Francisco? Was there more to his health problems and his Civil War wound than either had indicated? Nothing more was recorded.

I was curious to see the hot spring that Charles bathed in. I hadn't visited the one in Salt Lake City because it was hidden under a derelict building beside a six-lane highway, but I wondered if I could find this one, in the hills to the east of Santa Barbara. My research in the library had revealed that it must be the Montecito Hot Springs, which was being used by the Chumash Indians at least seven thousand years ago. The spring became quite a tourist resort in the 1880s, and then an exclusive club, but it burned down in the Coyote Wildfire in 1964 and was abandoned. The helpful library staff told me not to worry about the No Trespassing signs; the current owners were happy for people to walk on the trails, but put signs up so as not to establish a legal precedent.

After looking for a good topographical map of the whole area but having to make do with a street map of Santa Barbara and neighboring Montecito, I set off later in the afternoon than I had intended. I found wealthy Montecito easily enough and cycled uphill through the exclusive gated properties, past one especially high gate with a scary sign aimed at potential intruders saying "Warning: Armed Response." Montecito residents are said to include fifteen billionaires.

When I got to the parking lot with access to the Hot Springs Canyon trail, there was another scary poster saying "Beware! Several documented encounters with aggressive mountain lions lately. If you must hike, do so with a buddy." It suggested filling your pockets with stones to scare them. I didn't have a buddy, but I wasn't going to give up after coming that far, so I filled my pockets with stones and carried on, leaving my bike locked to the fence.

The rough, rocky path through the chaparral was hard going, winding haphazardly upwards past sandstone boulders and under oaks and sycamores. I turned around to look back at the deep blue Pacific Ocean, framed by the slopes of the canyon, which also nicely hid the large Montecito mansions. Further on, my heart suddenly leapt at the sound of a growl, and I whipped around. According to the sign, mountain lions are silent and attack from behind. I saw nothing anywhere, and I breathed a sigh of relief. I also worked out that what I thought was a growl was actually the sound of an insect dive-bombing past the microphone of my hearing device.

I met a tall man in shorts coming down the trail and we chatted. He said he had seen no sign of mountain lions, but he had his dog with him. I explained my goal. "Wrong season, I'm afraid," he said. "They are dry at this time of year. Why don't you visit a cold spring instead, just over there?" He pointed. As the sun was low in the sky, and a mountain lion was lurking in the back of my mind, I took his advice and, sadly, never made it to the site of the hot springs.

Since my visit, much has happened. The Santa Barbara Land Trust raised 7.8 million dollars from local individuals, families, and

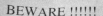

BEWARE !!!!!!

SEVERAL DOCUMENTED ENCOUNTERS WITH
AGGRESSIVE MOUNTAIN LIONS LATELY.

IF YOU MUST HIKE, DO SO WITH A BUDDY.

NO DOGS OR CHILDREN. THEY ATTRACT
MOUNTAIN LIONS.

IN ALL OF THE RECENT ENCOUNTERS, THE
LION(S) COULD BE SCARED AWAY BY
THROWING ROCKS AT THEM. HOWEVER,
HAVE THE ROCKS IN YOU POCKETS. YOU
MAY CAUSE THE LION TO POUNCE IF YOU
BEND DOWN TO PICK UP STONES, BECAUSE
IT MAKES YOU LOOK SMALLER.

HOWEVER, YOU MAY NEVER SEE THEM
UNTIL TOO LATE. THEY PREFER TO ATTACK
FROM BEHIND.

FOR DETAILS OF RECENT ENCOUNTERS, OR
TO REPORT AN INCIDENT, CONTACT JAMES
POWELL  805-969-0730

COYOTE@WEST.NET

*When I went looking for the Montecito Hot*
*Springs that my grandfather probably visited, I*
*was warned about mountain lions, but I filled*
*my pockets with stones and carried on.*

foundations to buy this land and then handed it over to the Forest Service for long-term stewardship, so these trails are now officially open to the public. I don't know if mountain lions are still lurking there, but the hot springs story may not be finished. The gist is that the Friends of Montecito Hot Springs have tried, and failed, to get the springs opened back up for the public to use. An obscure tax-exempt organization called the Montecito Creek Water Company has held the legal rights to 50 percent of the spring water since 1897 as well as the previous owners' permission to take the remaining 50 percent, so all the water, which is not drinkable, is diverted to a few Montecito homeowners for irrigation of their lawns.

Requests to get the Forest Service to reclaim 50 percent of the water for the public have gone unheeded. Attempts by someone to make pools for bathing (on public land, but filled from the water company pipes) have been destroyed. Posts on a Facebook page rumble on in anger. I think it would be a public-spirited gesture to make a hot spring available, and it irks me that the privileged residents insist on being selfish.

It was well after dark when I finally got back to Robert and Deby's house. Although they had told me they went to bed at dusk, they were still up. "We were worried about you," they said. "You lost your bike, then your precious briefcase, so we thought perhaps you'd lost yourself!" I chose not to mention the mountain lions.

---

For Charles and Fannie, the evenings between Christmas and New Year's Day, spent with the other hotel guests, sounded increasingly lively. Fannie wrote about how enjoyable one evening had been after a day of constant rain: "Stories, conundrums etc. Laughed quite as much as was healthy for us." New Year's Eve was a Sunday, so their day included the usual church activities, with a Presbyterian service in the morning, singing Sunday School hymns in the afternoon, and a Methodist service in the evening. (Fannie's diary for 1872 is missing, so I only have Charles' records from this point.)

On New Year's Day, Charles and Fannie stayed in during a rainy morning and wrote letters, but when it cleared in the afternoon, they went to the beach with friends to collect shells, and then spent a quiet evening in the parlor, playing checkers and backgammon.

A few days later, a party including Charles and four other men went off with a local huntsman for some serious small game hunting, and came back with quail, snipe, ducks, and hawks, having had "a grand and jolly time." The next day, one of the wives served the game for breakfast, "nicely cooked with most luscious coffee and broiled ham and fried cakes." Another wife remarked, "It was a 'Rooster party.' Gentlemen without their ladies."

As well as engaging in their typical leisure activities of beach-combing and hunting, the Rices went to see several nearby farms, which grew what to them were exotic fruits and vegetables. I thought that, as easterners from the merchant class, perhaps they were interested in how agriculture was developing in southern California. (I concluded while in Los Angeles that Charles had a more personal interest, which I will touch on later.) At Major Shaw's farm, Charles described huge beets, some weighing 100 pounds each, and peach trees in blossom. They picked hard-shelled almonds, and saw oranges, olives, and figs. And at Mr. Packard's, they toured orchards planted with orange, olive, almond, mulberry, and Japanese plum trees, as well as grapevines and an India rubber tree. It was unlike anything they'd ever seen in New England.

One of the reasons I particularly wanted to visit Santa Barbara was to explore its Spanish background. Any place in the United States with a Spanish history feels exotic to me, as a New Englander. I was excited to see the lovely terracotta tiled roofs and white adobe walls all through the center of town. I thought it odd that Charles and Fannie spent six weeks there and never mentioned the Spanish or recent Mexican history. They and the other guests at Lincoln House seem to have established a distant outpost of New England and ignored the Mexican culture around them. The only reference Charles ever made was when he recorded coming back from shooting eleven quail and stopped at the mission on the hillside for some cake and wine. They must have stopped because they were hungry, not to find out more about the local culture.

My research in the library suggested that Americans in Santa Barbara, whose nation had taken over the town twenty-five years earlier, in 1846, assumed the culture they brought with them was so superior that it rendered what they regarded as the inferior Spanish/Mexican presence invisible. When I had looked at the Presidio, I had noticed that it wasn't aligned with the streets around it but faced the street at an awkward angle. I learned that the reason for this was that one of the first things the newly arrived Americans did was survey the town to create an orderly modern grid system, and they set this down on top of the existing town, which had grown up haphazardly. (If their intention was to show the supposedly sloppy Mexicans how things ought to be done, it came unstuck. The survey chains included some oxhide that expanded and contracted during the day, thus creating numerous errors that are still reflected in a variety of awkward kinks and dog-legs in the grid system today.)

Unlike Charles and Fannie, I was keen to find out more about the Spanish and Mexican history of the American Southwest. I had made my first foray into the area in 2004 on Route 66, traveling through New Mexico, Arizona, and southern California, but I hadn't investigated the history. What were the differences in Spanish colonization compared to that of the British?

I learned that California, on the fringes of the Central American Spanish Empire until 1769, didn't have enough willing settlers, so the Spanish used their mission system there, which was a method of securing colonial frontiers by Christianizing the indigenous people and using them to provide a labor force. Religious orders did the Christianizing and the military kept control with forts (presidios) and small civilian colonies (pueblos).

The stated aim was to educate the Indians to become Spaniards and then transfer them to the civilian pueblo so the mission could move on to new areas. The Indians didn't seem to want to become Spaniards, preferring to return to their own homes, if possible. So the transfer to pueblos never happened and the missions continued to expand, thanks to their supply of, essentially, slave labor.

By the time Mexico gained independence from Spain in 1821, the Franciscan missions were very powerful, comprising churches, schools, farms, factories, and prisons and operating alongside a nearby presidio and pueblo. Newly independent Mexicans with aspirations wanted to reduce the power of the missions and coveted the vast lands they held. The missions were secularized in 1834, which meant all the mission land was redistributed. Half was to go to the Indians, but in practice, distribution was haphazard. Indians were often swindled out of it or were simply never told they owned any. But the Mexican government did distribute more than five hundred land grants to prominent Californio families (who were California-born but of Spanish descent, more or less), some of whom already had land through existing mechanisms, such as land grants given to retiring colonial soldiers. During what is known as the Rancho Period, extensive cattle rancheros were created along the California coast and in the Sacramento valley to supply the hide and tallow industries by ship to Boston. Apparently, a number of New Englanders were early settlers in Mexican Santa Barbara, having arrived on ships from Boston as a result of this trade.

For several years after the American takeover, the local Californio cattle industry continued to thrive because of the Gold Rush in the 1840s and 1850s, but in the 1860s a flood, a drought, and dwindling demand for beef products caused a crisis for the rancheros. Despite promises made at the end of the Mexican-American War, the rancheros were forced by US courts to prove entitlements to their lands. Unable to pay taxes, mortgages, legal fees, and other mounting debts, and at times mystified by the American legal system, rancheros began to lose their holdings by default or were forced to sell land at rock-bottom prices. The result was a huge transfer of wealth into American—or Anglo, as they were known—hands.

A speculative land boom and the beginnings of tourism saw everlarger numbers of Anglos arrive in the late 1860s and early 1870s. The area acquired a reputation as a health resort and many who came for a cure stayed on. In 1870, Anglos became the majority and, by the mid-1870s, Santa Barbara was primarily an American town.

Californios were gradually being displaced by Anglos, but they didn't disappear. Santa Barbara City Council was created in 1850 and a Californio was the first mayor. In 1864, the council selected Spanish as the official language for all their public records. Not until Anglos finally outnumbered Spanish speakers in 1870 was it replaced by English.

Pablo de la Guerra, whose hacienda I had cycled by, was a prominent Santa Barbara Californio. The de la Guerra family was powerful in New Spain and then Mexico and had probably obtained more land when the missions were secularized. After the Americans gained control, Pablo de la Guerra quickly adapted to the new situation. Getting involved in American politics, he was a delegate to the first constitutional convention of California in its bid for statehood, and went on to be elected to the state senate. In 1869, when he ran for district judge, his opponents challenged his right to office on the grounds that

Congress had failed to grant citizenship to de la Guerra or other Californios. In a landmark case in 1870, the California Supreme Court upheld de la Guerra's right to run for public office, saying that when California was admitted as a state, former Mexican nationals had become citizens.

The 1870 census shows Pablo and Josefa de la Guerra living with their seven children on East de la Guerra Street, so the family would have been there when Charles and Fannie visited, although it's most unlikely they met. I thought it was a shame that my great-grandparents weren't curious about the people whose land had been taken over by the Americans, when they had been curious about the Chinese in San Francisco. Perhaps the Californios' Catholicism put them off. Or maybe it never occurred to them that they would have had anything in common with the de la Guerra family. I'm sure Charles would have been interested, and surprised, to know that Pablo de la Guerra supported the Union cause during the Civil War, and was involved in the creation of Company C of the California Cavalry Battalion, whose members were mostly from the de la Guerra family and spoke no English.

The Casa de la Guerra, I discovered, was holding an open house, so I went along. I met Dibblee Hoyt, one of Pablo de la Guerra's direct descendants, and told him I wished Charles and Fannie had met his ancestor. He didn't seem nearly as interested in the history as I was. The de la Guerra family now has a website "dedicated to the descendants of José de la Guerra y Noriega" (Pablo's father) and enjoys annual descendants' gatherings, sometimes at the Casa de la Guerra. Unlike indigenous Indians, Californios had some standing, and quickly became a part of the social mix of Californian society at all levels.

So what about the Spanish influence I could see all around me that Charles and Fannie hadn't even mentioned? Amazingly and ironically, they couldn't mention it, because most of it dates from around the 1920s, fifty years later. The rest of the nineteenth century saw Spanish/Mexican influence diminish, but as the twentieth century approached, the Anglos found a surprising well of nostalgia—they had come under the spell of a Californian version of Wild West myth-making that romanticized the earlier history.

It may have started with a novel by Helen Hunt Jackson, who was a liberal Californian determined to highlight the case of the badly treated Mexicans and Indians. In 1884 she wrote the novel *Ramona*, the story of a half-white, half-Indian girl who falls in love with an Indian; they elope, but then suffer terrible discrimination. Unfortunately, Jackson's attempt to support the Mexicans and Indians backfired. Her novel was immensely popular, but readers fastened on to her romantic depiction of the missions rather than the discrimination against the Indians. Boosters trying to transform southern California into the cultural and economic capital of the West saw the novel's vision of the Spanish past as a winner, characterizing the Indians as noble savages and the Americans as villains, and romanticizing the Spanish missions. Historian Carey McWilliams coined the term "fantasy heritage" in the 1940s, pointing out that it covered up the real history of the brutal forced labor system of the missions.

A damaging earthquake in 1925 coincided with this thinking and led to Santa Barbara being rebuilt with a unified Spanish character in the Colonial Revival style. Some adobe houses still remaining in Santa Barbara were built before the American takeover in 1848. Most of those were bought by Anglos in the 1920s and restored. The magnificent Spanish/Moorish Santa Barbara County Courthouse was built in 1929, and the Arlington Theatre, designed to provide patrons with the illusion of being under the open sky in the courtyard of a Spanish village, was built in 1931. Santa Barbara has an annual Old Spanish Days Fiesta, which started in 1924.

It seems I had fallen into the trap of exploring a mainly invented Spanish Santa Barbara history—but I have to confess that the atmosphere and visual treats of that setting are still a winning formula, and I was hooked. I told myself I could appreciate it as long as I also acknowledged that it didn't represent the real past. I also thought about the adobe houses from the Spanish/Mexican period that are unlikely to have survived if they had not been restored by American owners in the early twentieth century.

The fantasy heritage disguised the real mission history, but the sources of the nostalgia in Santa Barbara were more complicated. The Southwest of the United States that was once Spanish, then Mexican, and then American came out of a complex intertwining, through contact and marriage, of Spanish, Mexican, and American cultures that were very different. For one thing, the Spanish pleasure principle softened the staid Yankee self-denial.

The 1920s fashion for the Spanish look did cause some casualties. Chinese tenants in the de facto Chinatown clustered around the old Presidio were evicted and the buildings knocked down, all to restore the earlier Spanish look. Some Santa Barbara residents were unhappy that many Chinese were leaving and encouraged a New Chinatown to rise about a block away, further along East Canon Perdido Street. Jimmy Yee Chung opened Jimmy's Oriental Gardens restaurant there in 1947. It closed in 2006 and is now in the hands of the Trust for Historic Preservation, and one part of it will become a museum of the Santa Barbara Chinese and Japanese communities' history.

I didn't want to leave Santa Barbara, but it was time to catch the train to Los Angeles. I decided that I wouldn't risk checking in my bike on this stretch, but I also wouldn't carry it all the way to my coach seat, which was bound to be at the end of the long train. I wheeled my bike onto the platform and was immediately stopped by an Amtrak employee who asked me what was I doing, saying bicycles weren't allowed. I explained that it was a folder, and that I was going to wheel it along and then dismantle it when I got to my coach. She looked doubtful, but let me continue.

As the train pulled out of the station, I was admiring the Spanish-looking architecture when I suddenly noticed some trolleys stacked along the wall. Trolleys for baggage! Trolleys that I could have put my folded-up bike, panniers, and backpack on! It was the one and only time that I saw any trolleys at any station on the whole of the Amtrak network I traveled on—and I hadn't seen them in time to use them. (Why weren't they stacked near the entrance to the station?)

WITH FRIENDS they had made at Lincoln House, the Rices left Santa Barbara on January 15, 1872, boarding the Orizabu steamer at dusk and disembarking the next day, one hundred miles further south, in San Pedro Harbor. Their journey continued on the new San Pedro Railroad for twenty-one miles to Los Angeles, a ramshackle town of five thousand people with great aspirations.

They stayed for two weeks at Pico House on Los Angeles Plaza in the town center, joining still more friends already there whom they had met in Santa Barbara. Said to be the most lavish hotel in Southern California, Pico House was built in 1870 by Pio Pico, who had been the last Mexican governor of California during the Mexican-American War. He was another elite Californio who scrambled on to the economic bandwagon of the new rulers and became a successful businessman and rancher, with more than a quarter of a million acres of land, although later he lost his money and ended his life in near poverty. Pico House was built in the Italianate style, also called American Romanesque, with eighty rooms, a richly planted central courtyard and fountain, and a winding staircase. It is still in the middle of Los Angeles, recently restored.

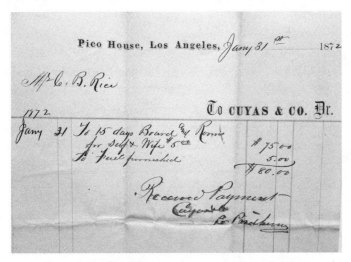

*In Los Angeles, the Rices stayed at Pico House, owned by Pio Pico, who had been the last Mexican governor of California during the Mexican-American War.*

In Los Angeles, Charles and Fannie were confronted with more of the Spanish-Mexican element than in Santa Barbara. Pico House was not only Mexican-owned but was probably staffed by Mexicans, so they were staying in the antithesis of the New England clapboard boarding house in Santa Barbara.

Their first excursion with some other couples into what Charles described as "beautiful" countryside was to San Gabriel Mission, eighteen miles north of Los Angeles. (It is now swallowed up in the urban sprawl, but is still there.) Charles described it as an Indian settlement, although it was still a functioning Catholic mission. Perhaps he was comparing it to the Dolores Mission in San Francisco, which had lost its Indian workforce much earlier because it was in urbanized San Francisco.

San Gabriel was established in 1771, the fourth of the Spanish missions in California, and played an important part in Los Angeles' economic development by showing that citrus could be grown successfully there. The Indians who lived in a village surrounding the mission were called "Gabrielenos" by the Spanish, but their true name was the Tongva.

Back in the center of Los Angeles, Charles and Fannie visited Sonora Town, so-named because initially it was the area where many gold miners from Mexico's Sonora area had ended up after returning from the Gold Rush. It was occupied by subsequent groups of new arrivals like the Chinese, but it kept the name. The area around Los Angeles was closer to the rest of Mexico and much flatter than the area further north, so it had seen more settlement from Mexico by people who were generally part Indian, part African, and part Spanish, descendants of soldiers who had received small land grants when they retired.

Charles concluded, "The Spaniards as a class here are a ruffianly set of men, mostly gamblers." Reading this, I conclude that tourists everywhere and through the years jump to conclusions and generalize. I try not to, but I'm probably guilty of it, too.

Los Angeles was still raw, in the uncertain transition of becoming American, with diverse groups rubbing up against each other. The diversity was more "in your face." Charles didn't mention (he probably wasn't told) that, about six months earlier (a few days before the Rices arrived in San Francisco), five hundred mostly white men killed eighteen Chinese in what became known as the Chinese Massacre of 1871. This fight over a contested marriage to a Chinese woman turned into a riot, starting in the Calle de los Negros and spilling over into La Plaza, near Pico House. Only one of the Chinese who was evenutally killed was involved in the original fight. More evidence of onlookers jumping to unwarranted conclusions . . .

As in Santa Barbara, Charles and Fannie made a point of visiting large farms during their two-week stay. Some were owned by new arrivals from other parts of the United States, who were buying land cheaply from the struggling Californios. On the way back from the San Gabriel Mission, the Rices visited the one-thousand-acre farm of Leonard Rose, with orange trees, grapevines, and numerous walnut and almond trees. Rose, who came to the United States from Germany when he was a child, had moved to Los Angeles in 1860 to grow citrus and grapes in what is now eastern Pasadena. He attributed his success to choosing land in the foothills that had springs and didn't need irrigation. A few days later the Rices saw more orange and walnut orchards, vineyards, strawberries, and even some "Sicily Lemon trees . . . almost large enough for bearing."

——

CHARLES' ENTRIES in his diaries over the years have led me to believe that the family history handed down orally by my uncle wasn't quite the same story that I have detected in the diaries. Some of my conclusions, however, are more about reading between the lines than what he actually wrote.

Charles became a grain merchant thanks to the opportunity presented to him by his father-in-law, but I don't think he was happy in that job, and I believe he harbored a desire to go into farming. He might have discussed this with Fannie, but probably no one else.

Traveling through the homesteading states of Illinois and Iowa, he had mentioned the attractiveness of the land if he were to take up farming, and in California he had made a point of visiting farms. Before he went on to set up in the grain business independently of his father-in-law in 1876, he investigated buying a farm in Virginia, but it came to nothing. His visit to Virginia was just a few months after he had taken out a life insurance policy following some bouts of illness, so he must have been worried about his health. But he must also have been desperate to break off his partnership with his father-in-law, and he hoped to do it through farming.

After he was diagnosed with TB in 1879, he spent winters in the south and summers in Vermont. During one summer in Brattleboro, he bought some sheep with the intention of breeding them for their merino wool. He got ill again and had to sell them.

My uncle always described the position Charles got in Alabama in 1882 rather grandly as "the Treasurer of Talladega College." (He got the job via the American Missionary Association in New York, and was paid by them.) To my astonishment, Charles' diaries showed that his main job there was that of farm manager—being treasurer just involved some bookkeeping. I suspect that my uncle was caught up in a Crosby family tradition of snobbery, thinking that farming was beneath the status of a merchant. Or to be more charitable, perhaps the Crosbys just felt that buying and selling commodities was more up-to-date and that farming was old-fashioned. It's possible Charles didn't even tell his in-laws that he was more of a farm manager than a college treasurer. Whatever the truth, it seems that Charles felt obliged to downplay his interest in farming. I was pleased to discover this information; I take delight in overturning family myths. Perhaps it is my contribution to historical revisionism.

---

T HE NEXT DAY was Sunday, so of course the Rices went to church, to the Congregational Church in the morning and the Episcopal Church in the evening. On Monday they visited Joseph Wolfskill's farm. Not all the farms in the area belonged to new arrivals from American states. A significant number of men had come to the area when it was Mexican, had become Mexican citizens, and had integrated into the society, with any luck managing to marry into wealthy Californio families. William Wolfskin, Joseph's father, was one of those. He had gone from Missouri to Los Angeles in 1831 and married

Magdalena Lugo, from a wealthy Californio family. He started the farm in 1844. He is credited with starting the California commercial citrus-growing business by selling oranges during the Gold Rush with fruit from saplings obtained from San Gabriel Mission. When Charles and Fannie visited, the Wolfskill farm had citrus, date-bearing palms, strawberries, grapes, vineyards, walnuts, and almonds. (By 1887, the city of Los Angeles was next door, so the land was valuable real estate and the family sold it off as building lots. It is now underneath a nondescript area of warehouses near the center of Los Angeles.)

A few days after that visit, on a windy day with dust flying everywhere, the Rices went back to San Gabriel Mission, where they were impressed by two date-bearing palm trees about seventy-five feet tall, and by a plant that Charles said had grown twenty-five feet in six weeks. (Charles named it, but his writing is illegible). They also visited Benjamin Davis Wilson's orange orchard with "six hundred trees loaded with fruit." Wilson was another American who had come to the area when it was Mexican. As well as developing orchards, he bought and sold land; he was made the Justice of the Peace for keeping track of local Indians; and he was elected mayor of Los Angeles and later a state senator.

Then the Rices rode past General Stoneman's ranch: "three hundred acres for which he paid twelve thousand dollars." They had been introduced to General Stoneman, a Civil War veteran, on their first day in Los Angeles. His ranch, Los Robles (The Oaks), is now underneath the long, straight, suburban North and South Robles Avenues in Pasadena.

Farming in California never resembled the model seen in the Midwest or the Plains, where homesteaders could acquire cheap government land for small family farms. Californian farming has always been large-scale. The best land for farming and ranching was originally part of the missions, and then was held within the large old Mexican land grants that were challenged in the American courts over many decades and mostly transferred to Anglos who had money.

Charles and Fannie soon went on another outing on horseback—to Asphaltum Springs, now better known as the La Brea Tar Pits. Tar pits are springs of molten asphalt, a residual form of petroleum. The tar was used by Chumash Indians to waterproof their boats, and white settlers used it to seal their roofs. Prehistoric animals were trapped in the tar and their remains were later found by employees of an oil company that drilled there starting in the late 1870s, but their significance wasn't recognized until about thirty years later. The site, in the middle of built-up Los Angeles, is now the Page Museum, which continues to excavate the pits and displays more than three million Ice Age specimens, including saber-toothed cats, dire wolves, and mammoths.

It was time to return to San Francisco, so some shopping with friends was in order. Charles bought a saddle and bridle to take home. He also bought an orange tree sprout for a cane for his father-in-law that cost fifty cents, and some photographic views of Los Angeles. He and Fannie attended an evening minstrel show with eight other friends, but it was "a miserable performance. Cost one dollar per ticket." I suspect he thought the acting was poor, rather than the show offensive. Minstrel shows, with white people dressing up as blacks and making fun of them, seemed to be acceptable then. I'm quite sure my great-grandparents were unaware of any problem, but it makes me wonder what unthinking prejudices I might reveal to future observers.

# 9

# BACK IN SAN FRANCISCO FOR THE CHINESE NEW YEAR

*Thursday Feby 8, 1872. Rainy nearly all day. This is the commencement of the Chinese Year and they are having a holiday. Stores closed. Calling upon each other. Worshipping in their temples. Rev Mr. Eills, Dan P Eills and myself visited one of their Joss Houses and the Chinese Young Men's Christian Association rooms where we drank tea and partook of Chinese confectionery with them.*

—Charles' diary

RETURNING to San Francisco, Charles and Fannie booked a room in the Occidental Hotel instead of the Grand. Some years earlier, Mark Twain, who was visiting San Francisco from the Nevada silver mines, where he was failing to make his fortune, showed his superior talent with words in describing the Occidental Hotel:

To a Christian who has toiled months and months in Washoe; whose hair bristles from a bed of sand, and whose soul is caked with a cement of alkali dust; whose nostrils know no perfume but the rank odor of sage-brush—and whose eyes know no landscape but barren mountains and desolate plains; where the winds blow, and the sun blisters, and the broken spirit of the contrite heart finds joy and peace only in Limburger cheese and lager beer— unto such a Christian, verily the Occidental Hotel is Heaven on the half shell. He may even secretly consider it to be Heaven on the entire shell, but his religion teaches a sound Washoe Christian that it would be sacrilege to say it.

—Letter to the Virginia City Territorial Enterprise, June 1864

The Rices' change to the Occidental was probably because it was much cheaper—$3.00 per person per day instead of $4.50. California prices were higher than those in the East, and the state didn't deal in paper money, insisting on gold, so Charles had to request drafts of dollars to be sent from Brattleboro for purchasing the gold. The paper-to-gold rate was never to his advantage: "Got $400.00 check. Cashed at Bank. Proceeds $364.00 gold . . . Received letter from home dated Feby 19th containing draft $300.00 currency. Sold it to Mr. Kellogg for $273.00 Gold." He didn't complain in his diary, but he must have been miffed.

Their lives returned to the routine they had established earlier, but with the added interest of invitations from men they had met at the Congregational Church Sunday School to attend celebrations of the Chinese New Year. It was a novel experience for them to be served tea in tiny cups without milk or sugar. Charles was particularly impressed with one of the Chinese New Year rules—that all debts must be paid before the New Year and new clothes made ready to put on—and he said white people would do well to copy it. He also recorded that he had "made an appointment to visit a Chinaman at 10 A.M. tomorrow."

The next day started with "drinking wine and tea with Chow Chong," who must have been the man he had arranged to see. He also recorded that he and friends had listened to someone reading from the Bible, had visited another Joss House, and had then gone to a Chinese restaurant, again with Chow Chong. Charles added, "We read *Great Expectations* in the evening." I smiled at the contrast between a day with the Chinese and an evening with Dickens.

Another evening, Charles and two friends went to a performance of a Chinese theatre troupe. Through my research, I learned that these were a valued way for the Chinese who were far from home to keep in touch with historical and moral teachings. They were also social occasions. Plays went on for hours, with much coming and going and conversations taking place. Charles recorded, politely, that half an hour was long enough to stay—"the music is a jargon and the acting and conversation being in Chinese one cannot understand it."

Charles wrote that "like the white race, the Chinese have their weaknesses and many bad men are to be found among them, but I

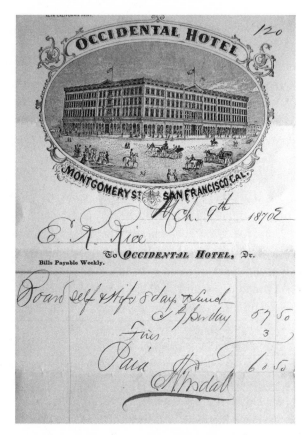

*When the Rices returned to San Francisco, they
stayed at the cheaper Occidental Hotel.*

think not more, if as many, as among the whites." He had been scathing about the Indians and the Mormons, so I wondered why he was so much more tolerant and accepting of the Chinese. His views must have arisen out of his participation in the Congregational Church. He was made a trustee of the Brattleboro Centre Congregational Missionary Society branch in 1869, probably because of his experiences in the Civil War and with slavery. The American Missionary Association (AMA) had been founded in 1846 by East Coast Congregationalists unhappy with the racism of many missionary boards. The AMA didn't organize churches—it founded schools. Before and after the Civil War it had functioned as an effective evangelical/abolitionist educational agency for blacks in the South. It also became interested in American Indians and immigrants from China and Japan.

Charles and Fannie were also responding to the ministry of Andrew Stone, minister at the Congregational Church in central San Francisco. Dr. Stone was a charismatic preacher, who often preached at the San Francisco Pavilion Skating Rink. Charles had commented on the surprisingly large audience at one of these prayer evenings.

Located on the edge of Chinatown, the Congregational Church offered Sunday School classes to the Chinese community, which introduced the Rices to the other side of the mainstream story. My quibble is that Congregationalists admitted without the slightest qualm that they were "baiting the Gospel hook with the English alphabet." Their overriding aim was to convert the Chinese to Christianity, since they were convinced it was the only way to save their souls. I needn't have worried. Although many converted to Christianity, most continued to worship their Chinese gods as well. At a meeting of the Chinese Young Men's Christian Association, Charles recorded one speaker saying: "Come over in Ship Nevada to dig gold. Found something better than dig gold in the earth—found this blessed Bible." It sounds like the young man was saying what he thought they wanted to hear. The Chinese appreciated the kindness and goodwill of the missionaries and were eager to learn English in the Sunday Schools. Perhaps converting was a small price to pay—and why not hold on to the backup plan?

It used to be said that the Chinese emigrations to California were a result of problems and poverty in China, but research has since shown that the Pearl River Delta region of Guangdong, from which they came, had already developed a market economy; people were traveling to find work, and trade was going on between California and China. When young men in China heard from traders about the discovery of gold, they responded like young men in America and Europe and came to find their fortunes. They also brought with them sophisticated social and cultural traditions that enabled them to survive the hostility they encountered.

Americans' belief that Christianity was God's plan may have led missionaries to try to save non-Christians by conversion to Christianity, but the accompanying assumption of white superiority led many other Americans to express outright hostility and prejudice about the foreigners and to attempt to get rid of them. Present-day California prides itself on its progressive political stances, but anti-Chinese prejudice in nineteenth-century California was extremely virulent.

Resentment toward foreign miners led the California State Legislature to pass a foreign miners' tax, making it difficult for Mexicans and Chinese to continue prospecting. The Chinese used their strong mutual benefit societies for support, bought up old claims, and worked abandoned tailings. Through a team effort, they were able to make a living where individual American miners could not. The Chinese also worked in quicksilver, borax, and other mines as laborers, and by 1870, one third of the miners in California were Chinese.

Central Pacific Railroad construction managers noticed the strength of the Chinese work ethic, and in the 1860s, they successfully recruited from China; but when the railroad was completed in 1869, it left twenty thousand Chinese unemployed. Some found jobs tending crops such as rice, oranges, apples, cherries, and peaches. Others filled the need for domestic services in white homes. They also went into business, opening laundries, restaurants, fishing and shrimping companies, and leather goods manufacturers. As soon as their new businesses flourished, however, they were targeted as unwelcome competition in the struggling economy of San Francisco and other parts of California. Californians had thought the railroad would bring prosperity, but it brought cheaper Eastern goods instead, and a recession followed in 1873.

Under the racist slogan "Chinese must go!," a campaign arose that tried to drive them out of the country. It became almost impossible for Chinese to become Americans. Men weren't allowed to bring their families over, so the Chinese population was mostly male, which led to a thriving brothel business. Many who settled in western towns were forced to flee to the Chinatowns on the coast for safety and support, but were isolated from the rest of the population, making it difficult, if not impossible, to assimilate into mainstream society. They were then criticized for being unassimilable.

The state of California passed numerous dreadful laws. There are too many to list, but here is a sample: excluding Chinese children from schools; banning Chinese from being admitted to hospitals; prohibiting Chinese, Indians, and blacks from testifying against whites in court; and banning their hair queues (pigtails) and their use of poles for carrying vegetables. Some of the laws were declared unconstitutional by courts, but then the legislators would try again with a variation.

It is ironic that, while the Chinese were being vilified, their understanding of plants used for medicinal purposes, much more advanced than Americans' knowledge at the time, became an important component of how injury and disease were treated in the nineteenth-century American West.

Some Chinese were also migrating in the other direction, to New York City, and in 1882, a draconian Chinese Exclusion Act was passed by Congress, the first law ever implemented to prevent a specific ethnic group from immigrating to the United States. It mocked the supposed American welcome to foreign immigrants. This law wasn't rescinded until sixty years later, in 1943, when the United States became allies with China against Japan.

So my great-grandparents, at whom I had been sniffing because of their many prejudices, were playing a significant part in a progressive movement of their time through their church. They may have perceived the world differently from me, but I have identified a thread that we shared. They had an ecumenical approach to religion, recognizing that different religions have lots in common and should work together on ways to help others and their communities. Back then, education was their way to be ecumenical, but these days ecumenicalism embraces churches' work on racism, poverty, sustainability, and many other issues that are important to me.

Reading up on the history of education, I learned that education for all still didn't exist back then. The provision of education was within the remit of state governments, so it varied across the country and was more advanced in the longer-settled East. Brattleboro had set up six school districts for the first time in 1782, and Isaac McCune, Fannie's great-grandfather, had been on one of the boards, overseeing one-room schools that taught reading, writing, and arithmetic. Cities, because they were expanding rapidly, were slower off the mark, especially in the West.

Sunday School, held on a day of no work, became a way for working children and older people to become literate. The teaching, no doubt, used Christian and Bible stories, but the outcome was learning to read and write. The 1871 San Francisco Directory entry for the First Congregational Church said that their Sunday School had five hundred scholars and teachers registered, and the average attendance was three hundred and eighty. Many more people attended Sunday School classes than went to church. Those in the late-nineteenth-century Sunday School movement campaigned hard for free state schooling so that they could concentrate on the religious aspects. Charles and Fannie may have felt that sharing their religious beliefs was paramount, but they also valued general education highly.

I saw frequent evidence of the value that Fannie placed on education in her early diaries. I discovered that she had even tried to go to college, but her attempt had been thwarted, presumably by ideas about a woman's place at the time. In 1867, one year after she married Charles, she wrote in her diary, "3 June: Wrote a letter to Julia telling her of my disappointment at being obliged to give up going to Vassar." (Vassar College, a women's college in Poughkeepsie, New York, was founded in 1861.) It impressed me that a married woman of those times would even consider going to college. Perhaps it is what was behind her dismay when, many years later, her son Howard, my grandfather, refused to go to college. He mentioned her feelings about his refusal, but without giving her reasons, in a short autobiography he wrote.

Andrew Stone, the Congregational Church minister, also valued education. The church Sunday School was a key aspect of his outreach work. He became one of the founders of the Pacific College, a theological seminary established in 1868. Charles mentioned the college several times, noting in his diary that Dr. Stone was appealing for funds to support it. Charles arranged to see someone to discuss it and then sent the college prospectus to his minister in Brattleboro. He obviously considered it worth backing.

Now calling itself the Pacific School of Religion, it is still going strong, located north of San Francisco on "Holy Hill" in Berkeley, along with several other religious seminaries. Its website says: "PSR was founded by Congregational ministers and laypeople, and funded by the historic congregations of the East and the emerging congregations of the West. The seminary was established on the traditions of New England Protestantism combined with the spirit of the western frontier, with a focus on democratic governance, educational excellence, and ecumenical cooperation."

Charles and Fannie's support for education was their way of looking outward from their faith. Their faith was also a major support for them in facing their own adversities. In early 1879, just six months after baby Howard was born, Charles went to a doctor in Boston, who examined his chest and said he had an "irritated larynx and seeming tenderness under the right clavicle sufficient to warrant a change of climate at once." He didn't record that it was consumption, now known as TB—but this was it, the dreaded diagnosis.

There had been hints of problems recorded in his and Fannie's diaries during the previous couple of years. On their eleventh wedding anniversary, in April 1876, Fannie wrote, "I tried to think of some way to celebrate but could not." In early 1877, after a few bouts of illness, Charles (but not Fannie) recorded that he had taken out a life insurance policy. Did Fannie know?

The day after the visit to the doctor, Charles and Fannie talked to their family doctor in Brattleboro, who advised a "carefully planned change." It took place a mere eight days later. On April 4, Charles went by train to Aiken, South Carolina, known for catering to people with consumption. Correspondence between Charles and Fannie took place almost daily. Fannie's diary entries were still brief, but showed her increasing desperation: "25 Apr—Had a doleful letter from Chas. He was much worse last Mon night and I am in despair over him . . . 26 Apr—Telegraphed Chas. Reply came that he is feeling better. Wrote him also . . . Am in despair as to what I am to do. 30 Apr—Decided to go to Chas . . . He needs me." She arranged for baby Howard, seven months old, to be looked after by someone in Worcester, and started on the five-day journey to Aiken.

On May 4 Charles wrote, "Another long lonesome day. Had to spend it in my room and mostly in bed not feeling strong enough to bear the burden of my clothes. As the day draws to a close a dread of the long night begins to possess me. Just now life is seemingly more of a burden than joy." Fannie finally arrived a few days later.

All this time, despite his ill health, Charles went to church every Sunday in Aiken. On one Sunday he attended the Colored Baptist and Methodist Church. This was in the South, just fourteen years after the Civil War, when Southerners were angry and bitter about losing the war and responding by building a racially segregated society. Charles didn't record the response by either whites or blacks to his attending the black church. He must have known that it wasn't considered socially acceptable, but he chose to persist.

Fannie stayed with Charles for a week, but then a crisis arose back home. Fannie's father urged them both to come home, without being clear about the reason. It took them five days in all, using a sleeper to Charleston, a berth on a steamer to New York City, and a train to Brattleboro. As it turned out, Edward Crosby had somehow discovered that Howard wasn't being looked after properly in Worcester and brought him home to Brattleboro. Fannie wrote, "He looked so sick when we saw him that it almost broke my heart."

Charles and Howard, along with Fannie, spent the summer recovering in Brattleboro and then the three of them went to Aiken for the winter, maintaining this pattern for the next three years. Charles and Fannie's daughter Marion was born in July 1882. Charles then got the job as farm manager and treasurer at the black Talladega College in Alabama, returning to his family in Brattleboro in the summers with the family going to visit him at other times. It was hard for all of them. In autumn 1885, Charles became very ill and was brought back from Talladega to Brattleboro, where, sadly, he died in November.

Thinking about the religious faith that had sustained Charles and Fannie, I decided to attend a Unitarian service. When I started living in Britain in the 1960s, I had attended services in Unitarian churches from time to time, but life was busy and other priorities intervened. Later, I tried again, attending a few services, but I gave up again. I learned that British Unitarianism developed quite separately from the

American version, so perhaps it's not surprising that it didn't attract me. I was keen to try an American Unitarian church.

I checked out the websites of several churches in the San Francisco Bay area that seemed to be well attended and socially active, and went one Sunday to the First Unitarian Church in Oakland. The morning service was billed as "more traditional," with the afternoon service "a more lively worship arts celebration." Before the service, a "greeter" welcomed me, which I appreciated. There were about twenty-five people in the enormous church.

There was nothing wrong with the service, but it didn't ring any bells for me. I decided to see what the later one was like. It attracted quite a few more people, but I'm afraid I was put off by its happy-clappy singing and dancing approach. Maybe American Unitarianism had changed while I was living in Britain and lost its appeal for me. Or maybe I had changed.

I looked instead for a Transition Initiative group that dealt with concerns about climate change. Transition, an international movement that started in Britain in 2005, is about making the necessary transition to a low-carbon world by tackling climate and economic crises with local community solutions. One of the Bay Area groups was showing a documentary about an election candidate's "No Growth" policy, which appealed to me. The film was fascinating, and it was also great meeting like-minded people.

The movie posed the question of why economic growth is considered essential for achieving prosperity when it clashes with the inconvenient fact that we live on a finite planet. If everyone lived the way the average American lives, we would need something like three planets. It reminded me of Ellen MacArthur, the young British sailor who broke the world record in 2005 for the fastest solo circumnavigation of the globe, and who went to the local school where I live. She was horrified at seeing so much plastic waste swirling around her yacht when she was miles from anywhere, so on her return, she set up the Ellen MacArthur Foundation, which works to accelerate the transition to a "circular economy."

Unlike the current "take, make, dispose" model, the circular economy would decouple global economic development from finite resource consumption by using and reusing the same materials indefinitely. How sensible! The foundation's recent report about plastics shows that they need never become waste and outlines the steps needed to achieve this systemic shift.

The movie on "No Growth" was stimulating and made me think. I found myself wondering about the nineteenth-century contact between cultures in the southwestern United States, where celebration and enjoyment had mingled successfully with the work ethic. What's happening in the Transition movement has some similarities, in that people value community solidarity and personal relationships more than making money to maintain a consumer materialist lifestyle. Afterwards, I went back to a local member's house and heard about numerous exciting Transition environmental projects in the area. I decided I must join a local Transition group when I returned home.

---

In 1872 San Francisco, Charles and Fannie had a few days of good weather, but it rained practically every day for the rest of February. They spent time with friends, tramped around the wet streets looking for books, and read a lot. They also shopped, buying some carved ivory chessmen and dice boxes at Matzo's for twelve dollars. Washington's birthday, on February 22, was a good weather day, celebrated with a parade. That evening they went to another minstrel show, this time a "good performance of the Alhambra Minstrels." Many of their friends seemed to be leaving—Mr. Hanna was off to Honolulu, and the Eills were returning to the East.

On March 1, 1872, they went to see the Japan steamer sail and wrote letters to their Sunday School classes. On the same day, President Grant signed the Yellowstone Park Act, creating the first national park in the history of the world. The United States had recognized some years earlier that its most famous natural landmark, Niagara Falls, had been nearly ruined for visitors because every overlook was owned by a private landowner charging a fee, so it began the process of protecting sites by creating national parks.

National parks have been a great success with the public, but it is now generally recognized that the creation of the national parks was done at the expense of resident Indians. The parks were established to celebrate wilderness. Indians living in the park were deemed "not wilderness," and were gradually forced to move out. The last Southern Sierra Miwok Indian living in Yosemite National Park was Jay Johnson, a park employee and also a campaigner for Indian rights. In 1980, he was traveling on business for his tribe and visiting one of the Smithsonian museums in Washington when he looked at a display that said that no Indians were left in the park. He pointed out to the museum staff that he was still there. However, fifteen years later, when he reached the age of sixty-five and retired from park employment, he was forced to move.

A week after watching the steamer depart, Charles and Fannie went south again, this time for two weeks, to San Jose, Santa Cruz, and Pescadero, traveling by train to San Jose and stagecoach afterwards. They stayed at the elegant Auzerais House in San Jose, which was built in 1864 by John and Edward Auzerais, French brothers who had emigrated in 1849 and established a successful grocery business. After a few days exploring the town itself, they rode by horse to a quicksilver (mercury) mine called New Almaden.

These days, tourists visit sites that tell the stories of industrial history, so it is initially counterintuitive to discover that tourists once went to see sites of industries that were just beginning. Charles described in detail the process of reducing the ore, and they were given specimens of cinnabar and some crystals. Mining first began in these mountains in 1845, when a Mexican officer, Captain Andres Castillero, discovered that the vermilion rock used by the local Ohlone Indians to paint themselves and the walls of the Santa Clara Mission was cinnabar, an ore containing mercury, then used for processing silver. In 1871, this mine was a state-of-the-art enterprise, equivalent to the Silicon Valley businesses of today. More mines followed. When they were closed in 1976, the Almaden Quicksilver County Park and the New Almaden Quicksilver Mining Museum were established; the mines had come full circle and tourists started visiting again.

Life at the New Almaden mine was vividly sketched by Mary Hallock Foote, the wife of Arthur DeWint Foote, the resident engineer from 1876. Her work appeared in *Scribner's Monthly* magazine in 1878, and New Almaden also featured in her memoir *A Victorian Gentlewoman in the Far West* (unpublished until 1972), which was fictionalized by Wallace Stegner in his novel *Angle of Repose*. Stegner's book, which won the Pulitzer Prize for Fiction in 1972, is one of my favorite novels about the American West—a story of the ups and downs of a complex marriage that encompassed two opposing strands of western settlement—the exploiter/rugged individualist, personified by Arthur Foote, and the civilizer/community builder, personified by Mary Foote.

In San Jose, Charles noted that there had been an earthquake in the morning, the first they had felt since they had arrived in California. He didn't express any concern. Perhaps he had read an article in the *Alta California*, on November 10, 1871, just after they had arrived in the city, that included an extract from the annual report of the Surveyor-General of California. Based on his knowledge of archives recording earthquakes in California from 1769 to June 1871, the Surveyor-General confidently stated, "I am firmly of the opinion that the earthquakes of California are not so much to be dreaded as generally supposed. In fact, that they are far less dangerous to life and property than are the hurricanes of the south or the summer tornadoes of the north; and I have no doubt but that the inhabitants of San Francisco and other California cities may so construct their buildings of brick or stone as to feel a reasonable degree of confidence that they may stand, unless destroyed by fire or flood, until they shall crumble slowly beneath the wasting hand of time."

Back in San Francisco, two weeks later, Charles noted another earthquake, in the middle of the night, with a bit more emphasis. "Severe shock of earthquake at 2:30 A.M. this morning felt all through the state." He didn't know it, but it was one of the strongest ever recorded in California, and as big as the one that would cause such destruction twenty-four years later in San Francisco.

From San Jose, they visited the nearby Santa Clara Mission. Charles described the building, which had been established in 1777, with none of the critical innuendoes he had used when describing Mission Dolores in San Francisco. I wonder if Santa Clara Mission, which had been rebuilt in 1825, was decorated more benignly than the older Mission Dolores. It was destroyed by fire in 1929 and replaced. It's touching that the bells still ring faithfully each evening, as they have been doing since 1798, at the request of King Carlos IV of Spain.

San Jose is now part of Silicon Valley, birthplace of America's ultramodern high-technology economic sector. The orchards and crops the area was known for in the nineteenth century have been replaced by glass and steel buildings. I went through it on the train when I left San Francisco to visit Santa Barbara and Los Angeles—yet another place I had to miss for lack of time and hoped to return to.

Charles and Fannie left San Jose and continued southwest by stagecoach, thirty-five miles across the mountains to Santa Cruz on the coast. The Santa Cruz Mountains had extensive forests with impressive redwoods that were being cut down wholesale, following the war with Mexico. What was left around Santa Cruz was eventually saved by wealthy Victorians and, in 1902, the first state park in California was created in Big Basin, twenty miles northwest of Santa Cruz, most of it old-growth redwoods. Charles and Fannie visited the beach and went to the old Santa Cruz Mission on horseback. Then they turned north along the coast for thirty-eight miles by stage to Pescadero, on a "horrid road."

Pescadero, on former Mission Santa Cruz pasture given to a Californio in 1833, had rich, fertile valley soil that attracted settlers, and in the 1860s it was a prosperous town, surrounded by farms and lumber mills. The Rices stayed for several days at Swanton House, did more beachcombing, attended the Methodist Church service on Sunday, and then left the next day for the final fifty miles back to San Francisco.

I didn't have time to do the same circular tour of San Jose, Santa Cruz, and Pescadero, but I hoped to make a connection with my great-grandparents' story by cycling along part of their return stagecoach route to San Francisco from Pescadero. I had read that the Indians had traditionally used a path along the coast, and I was particularly keen to cycle on the famous Route 1. Built in the 1930s alongside the Pacific Ocean for 656 miles, it is a draw for anyone wanting to explore the coastline of the Pacific Ocean, and popular with cyclists as well as motorists. I set off for a hostel at Point Montara, twenty-five miles south of San Francisco, to stay for one night and come back the next day.

The first day was disappointing, partly because I had a nasty cold and the sky was gray, but also because the sprawling suburbs to the south of San Francisco seemed to go on forever. Route 1 was just a busy street with houses on both sides and no sign of the Pacific Ocean. In the last suburb, Pacifica, I was relieved to spot the Pacifica Visitor Information Center, assuming I would find relevant maps or leaflets there. I was puzzled to find nothing whatsoever, and staff who knew nothing about cycling or hiking. But my spirits were soon lifted by seeing a large Pacifica Council election poster displayed in a front yard: "Mary Ann for Pacifica."

When I left the Pacifica houses behind, the famous coastal Route 1 wasn't what I was expecting. Most American highways have a paved shoulder, which is handy for providing cyclists with some distance from vehicles. This highway had no shoulder at all, and it was narrow and busy. It reminded me of narrow winding roads in the British countryside. It was also uphill, and I hate cycling on a narrow road uphill because the strain of pedaling means I sometimes inadvertently wobble, making me worry that I will wobble into the path of a vehicle. I concentrated hard on not wobbling and pressed on. How many of the 656 miles that cyclists rave about would be like this?

I was approaching the infamous Devil's Slide, a coastal promontory where an unstable mountain ridge of Mount Montara descends to the ocean and the road is regularly washed out by landsides. They were blasting a tunnel through the mountain to replace the road (it was opened in 2013), but meanwhile it was definitely scary for cyclists. Was there spectacular scenery? I was so busy flinching at the passing trucks that I could only get a fraught glimpse, to my right, of a steep drop to the ocean—the water extending out to a distant horizon—and to my left, across the road, a steep slope upwards. The too-narrow road clung precariously to the mountain and it didn't feel like there was enough space for me.

It widened eventually, so I stopped for a much-needed rest and could actually savor the spectacular view out over the ocean, with no boats or ships in sight. I tried to work out what the odd metal shack balanced precariously on the top of a nearby rocky ridge overlooking the Pacific could be. It looked like the land around its foundation had been eroded away and it might topple down in the next storm. It turned out to be the remnants of a World War II bunker, part of the San Francisco Harbor Defense observation posts.

My destination, Point Montara, made up for the intimidating cycle ride; it was a beautiful spot on a craggy bluff above the Pacific. The hostel included a small lighthouse and several former Coastguard buildings, nestled in a large patch of rainbow-hued wildflowers surrounded by a picket fence. A couple of wind-blown cedars added a Japanese-y touch. The lighthouse reminded me of ones I knew on the Maine coast, and it turned out that this lighthouse started working not far from Maine, on Cape Cod in Massachusetts. For some reason it was later transported three thousand miles to Montara, in 1875, where ships were regularly being wrecked on the offshore rocks.

The hostel itself was small and cozy and I had the women's dorm to myself. After I had settled in, I went for a walk on the sandy paths winding through rocky cliffs and down to the beaches and coves below, where the surf boomed and foamed. The evening sun turned the sand to gold and the steep vegetation on the cliffs above it to a rusty red terracotta. The pine trees further up were an almost-black green. The colors were a striking contrast to the deep steely blue of the Pacific Ocean and the pale grey-green surf surging onto the beach. I tried to imagine Charles and Fannie's stagecoach journey through this area.

For my evening meal, there was only one place close enough to get to by bike, so that's where I ended up: El Gran Amigo Taqueria, a tacky roadside cafe where I attempted my rusty Spanish but was laughed at in English, and had a splendid meal served on a paper plate: rice, refried beans, guacamole, salsa, and cheese, with Mexican beer. The next morning, having breakfast at the hostel, I was chatting with a Canadian visitor, who said something about Zoom Airlines. I asked her to say it again, since my flight back to Britain was on Zoom. "It has gone bust," she said. And *that's* how I found out, not from the airline, that my flight home, two weeks later, was caput. (When I got home, ridiculously, I found a letter waiting for me!) Luckily, this chance

*The evening sun on the Pacific Coast below the Point Montara lighthouse.*

encounter enabled me to sort out an alternative in plenty of time: a flight on another cheap airline, recommended by the Canadian.

I also asked one of the hostel staff if he knew of any way to return to San Francisco other than on the scary Route 1. He told me about an off-road route on the flanks of Mount Montara, using the remains of the Old San Pedro Mountain Road—built for cars in 1913, but replaced, lower down, by Route 1 in 1937. My return trip was a delightful contrast to that of the previous day, one of the most memorable cycle rides I have ever done. The guy at the hostel gave me a rough map that showed the old road heading out of the small town of Montara and I managed eventually to find it, though there were more roads and tracks on the ground than on the map. (Whenever I need a detailed map outside Britain, I long for British Ordnance Survey maps. I've never come across maps anywhere else in the world that come close to Ordnance Survey maps for clearly showing the way on tracks and footpaths.)

I looked out for a large shrub called Montara manzanita, so-called because it only occurs around Mount Montara, but I missed it, probably because it wasn't the time for flowering. I could see plenty of

*The Old San Pedro Road, which is marvelous for bicycles, was
the main road along the Pacific coast from 1913 to 1937.*

the distinctive clumps of silvery-white pampas grass, but sadly, it's
an invasive nonnative species. It was imported from Bolivia in the
1950s and planted for erosion control on road cuttings up and down
the coast, but its introduction was a disaster. These days, volunteers
do their best to keep it under control. Pinyon and junipers were plen-
tiful, too.

Not having been maintained since 1937, the intermittently paved
road was sometimes only two to three feet wide because of washouts,
but it wound its way slowly up the prominent ridge, switchbacking
along the gentlest of gradients—bliss on a bicycle. The sun blazed
down from a cloudless sky, with a cooling breeze from the ocean.
The road continued to gain height, passing a signpost at a junction
with a track heading off to a peak, and the Old San Pedro Mountain
Road going straight ahead. Finally I reached the ridge, and the road
went down instead of up. Across several more miles of track thread-
ing through the chaparral on a succession of lower ridges, I could
see built-up Pacifica and the ocean. I rolled on, enjoying a relaxed,
slow free-wheel downward. It was midweek, and I didn't see a soul

on the whole journey. I reveled in it, imagining it was the road my great-grandparents' stagecoach went along.

When I got down to Pacifica, the San Francisco bedroom community with the unhelpful visitor center, a cyclist came alongside me and started up a conversation, asking if I was doing the entire Route 1. I laughed and told him about my previous day's experience. He was in his thirties and worked as a plumber in San Francisco, but he could only afford to live in Pacifica, and he seemed to make a habit of being helpful to out-of-town cyclists often doing the whole Pacific Coast route. He said, "Follow me, and I'll show you a much better way back to the city." I followed him onto a marvelous bike trail along the beach and waterfront, which I had not known about the previous day. Local knowledge makes such a difference. Pacifica felt a lot more friendly and welcoming.

When we got to his turnoff, he stopped and pointed to the string of streets I should use to get to the better route to San Francisco, and wished me well. They wound up through houses on the steep hillside to a ridge. His route was a treat, although I was a bit taken aback to find myself cycling along the four-lane Skyline Boulevard, and was even more surprised to find it empty of cars with only one other cyclist in sight—I took a photograph to prove it. (Most cars now use Interstate 280.)

*Another cyclist and I are the only people using the Skyline Boulevard, a major highway approaching San Francisco. Where are all the cars?*

It was only when I was back in Britain and beginning to write this book that I discovered I hadn't actually retraced any of that portion of my great-grandparents' route after all. I was so keen to cycle on Route 1 that I had failed to read Charles' diary carefully enough at the point at which they left Pescadero. He described going to Spanish Town (renamed Half Moon Bay in 1874) and then San Mateo. I hadn't noticed that San Mateo is inland from the coast, so the road turned east and then northwest along the eastern shore of the San Francisco Peninsula. There was no road whatsoever along the coast then. As I had a far better day than if I had followed their route, I was grateful for my mistake.

Back in San Francisco, Charles made an unsuccessful search in the Lone Mountain Cemetery for the grave of "Father's brother," Enos Crosby. Enos had gone to San Francisco, without his wife and children, to work in gold mining as a pump maker, but had died in 1850 after a short illness. I hoped I might find his records belatedly in the Lone Mountain Cemetery records online, but he was nowhere to be found. The remains in the Lone Mountain Cemetery were moved ten miles to the suburb of Colma in the 1920s to make way for new housing, so some records may not have survived. Then I discovered that Charles was probably looking in the wrong place, since the Lone Mountain Cemetery didn't open until 1854, four years after Enos died. He might have been buried in the Yerba Buena Cemetery, but that is long gone, and the records were destroyed in the 1906 fire. Last resting places in the heady days of San Francisco's boom didn't all last.

They were only back in San Francisco for two weeks before they set off again, this time to the north, by ferry, train, and stage. They were going to see more sights that were essential destinations for Victorian tourists, sights I'd never even heard of: the Calistoga geysers and the Petrified Forest. Calistoga is at the northern end of Napa Valley, which I have heard of because of its famous wines. Back then, Napa Valley wine growers were experimenting, and sometimes trying to pass off their wines as European, because no one believed Californians would be able to produce good wine. Charles and Fannie mentioned wine grapes being grown on farms near Los Angeles several times, but said nothing about what was happening in Napa Valley.

They didn't get to Calistoga until 9:00 P.M., staying at the Calistoga Springs House, where they had a freezing night under hotel blankets that were too narrow. The next day they set off at 7:00 A.M. to see the geysers. Charles wrote that the "celebrated Foss" was their driver, and his speed was nerve-racking. Author Robert Louis Stevenson, who several years later went to the hills of Calistoga on his honeymoon, also met Foss. At the end of his train journey across the country in 1879, he had found and eventually married the woman he loved. They couldn't afford ten dollars a week for the Calistoga Springs House, so they squatted in an abandoned bunkhouse at the old Silverado quicksilver mine. He kept a diary and used his observations for the book *The Silverado Squatters* (1884). Of coach driver Foss, he wrote, "Flinching travelers, who behold themselves coasting eternity at every corner, look with natural admiration at their driver's huge, impassive, fleshy countenance . . . " He also described speaking briefly to Foss on a telephone, his first experience of this new invention. (Foss eventually had an accident while driving wildly on these roads, and never drove the wagon again.)

Charles and Fannie enjoyed the geysers and went to the Petrified Forest the following day. Stevenson wrote about the Petrified Forest in the *Silverado Squatters*: "At length, in a lonely dell, we came on a huge wooden gate with a sign upon it like an inn. 'The Petrified Forest. Proprietor: C. Evans,' ran the legend. Within, on a knoll of sward, were the house of the proprietor and another smaller house hard by to serve as a museum, where photographs and petrifactions were retailed. It was a pure little isle of touristry among these solitary hills." Stevenson's notes on the landscape and scenery of these mountains and valleys provided much of the descriptive detail for his famous *Treasure Island* (1883). The area is now part of the Robert Louis Stevenson State Park.

Calistoga's geysers and the Petrified Forest are privately owned but can be visited for a fee. I was interested to discover that the geysers are part of the world's largest and most developed geothermal field that generates electricity from steam. The area has been generating electricity since the 1960s, and now provides just over six percent of the state's supply. A state law passed since I was there requires that

*This is the San Francisco souvenir spoon that Charles and
Fannie brought back from their trip and that I inherited.
The Golden Gate was the name given to the entrance to
the bay, featuring the sun setting on the horizon of the
Pacific Ocean, before the famous bridge was built.*

*Fannie and Charles
had their photos taken
at Bradley Rulofson
Photographers on
Montgomery Street in
San Francisco on
February 12, 1872.
Charles' photograph
is missing.*

fifty percent of California's electricity come from renewable sources by 2030. Keep ramping it up, California!

Charles and Fannie returned to San Francisco and renewed their usual pattern of seeing friends and going to church and prayer meetings. They also began to think about returning home. Charles recorded more purchases, including a watch charm for Fannie, the symbolic "Bear of California" holding a pearl. He also bought some Chinese curiosities weighing 170 pounds for forty-five dollars at Chin Lee's. (As I had to carry all my purchases on my bicycle, I only bought a tiny Japanese carved figure, which now sits next to some items in my house handed down to me through my mother's family: two Oriental carvings and an antique Chinese doll, which might possibly have been in that cache of curiosities bought at Chin Lee's.)

The Rices had their photographs taken at Bradley and Rulofson's; Fannie's is in the book, but Charles' is missing. In the 1872 Directory in the San Francisco Library, I found an advertisement for the photographers' studio, boasting that it had "the only elevator connected with photography in the world"—an odd claim, but perhaps elevators had just been invented.

Toward the end of April, the time approached for their final departure from San Francisco. Charles listed numerous visits to friends and also to the stock exchange. Sunday, April 21, was their last day at Dr. Andrew Stone's First Congregational Church. The next day they began their journey home, but immediately interrupted it with two more weeks of visiting attractions in central California.

# 10

# RETURN HOME VIA GOLD MINES
# AND YOSEMITE VALLEY

*Sunday April 22, 1872. Clear and pleasant. Church
morning and evening. Heard Dr. Stone. Chinese Sunday
School. Mrs. Arnor and Louisa with us. Gregory called. Also
Mrs. and Louisa Arnor. Bid friends at church good bye.*
—Charles' diary

CHARLES AND FANNIE left San Francisco the following morning
and retraced the route by which they'd arrived five months earlier along the San Francisco Bay tidal estuary. The estuary is the gateway eastward through the coastal mountain ranges to the Great Central Valley, which dominates central California.

They stopped in Sacramento and spent several days traveling
around by train or steamer and stagecoach before their trip to Yosemite Valley. Without her diary, I don't have Fannie's thoughts, but I suspect that these days were for Charles, as a businessman, to find out
more about the aftermath of the discovery of gold twenty-four years
previously. Might he also have been looking at opportunities for his
future career?

By evening, they arrived in Marysville, a thriving industrial city
forty-five miles north of Sacramento. He doesn't explain why they
chose Marysville, but I assume it was through his contacts in the grain
trade, because he visited a mill before he left there. Marysville was an
important town in the Gold Rush, and it was their base for the next
few days. In 1848, French immigrant Charles Covillaud had found
gold nearby and bought land (which became the town) on the Feather
River, a tributary of the Sacramento River and a stopping point for
riverboats taking prospectors looking for gold.

The town was named Marysville after Covillaud's wife Mary,

who was a survivor of the tragic Donner Party of 1846–47. It quickly became one of the biggest cities in California, with mills, ironworks, factories, machine shops, schools, churches, and two daily newspapers. It isn't better known in the present day because it had to build flood levees in 1875 that prevented any further growth, and it is now much smaller than Yuba City and Linda next door.

Charles didn't record in his diary whether they used trains or steamers, but it could have been either. People today would be surprised to know how much traveling in nineteenth-century America was done by water, not land. The Rices and some friends spent three weeks in 1870 traveling three thousand miles from Brattleboro to Quebec, Montreal, Toronto, Niagara Falls, Chicago, and St Louis, and one thousand miles of their traveling was on water—on Lake Champlain, the St. Lawrence River, Lake Ontario, Lake Erie, and the Mississippi River.

People also tend not to know how much water there is in central California, where the tidal estuary from San Francisco becomes the inland Sacramento and San Joaquin River Delta for rivers draining the Sierra Nevada. I certainly didn't know this. The delta covers over a thousand square miles interlaced with hundreds of miles of waterways, and because the waterways now have flood levees, much of it is below sea level. It has been called California's Holland.

The next day Charles and Fannie went from Marysville along the Yuba River for twenty miles eastward to see hydraulic gold mining at Sucker Flat. Charles doesn't say so, but hydraulic mining was an environmental disaster. It used high-pressure jets of water to dislodge rock, and the resulting water-sediment slurry was directed through sluice boxes to remove the gold. It washed rocks and sediment into the waterways and caused flooding and havoc for farmers, and it's why Marysville had to build the levees that restricted its growth. Hydraulic mining was finally banned by California courts in 1884. I'm relieved that they recognized the importance of regulating industry on behalf of the collective good.

The couple then passed through Rough and Ready (a town using President Zachary Taylor's nickname) to spend the night in Grass Valley, a rich gold-mining district. Perhaps they stayed at the

Holbrooke Hotel, still there today and claiming to be "the oldest hotel in continuous operation in California's Mother Lode." Notable guests at the Holbrooke included Bret Harte, Jack London, Mark Twain, and several American presidents.

The gold-mining era still has some surprises for us. A California couple on their daily walk with their dog near this area a few years ago discovered what may be the greatest buried treasure ever found in the United States. The cache of rare Gold Rush–era coins was worth more than $10 million. Called the Saddle Ridge Horde, the 1,400 gold pieces, in nearly mint condition, were discovered buried in eight decaying metal cans on the couple's land.

The following day Charles and Fannie visited the nearby Eureka Mine, part of the extensive hard rock gold mine holdings of Empire-Star Mines, Ltd., developed by entrepreneurs after the easy surface placer gold had been exhausted by individual prospectors. Charles was taken down a shaft seven hundred feet deep, where he obtained a specimen of quartz that contained gold. The gold ore was brought to the surface, crushed in a massive stamping mill, combined with quicksilver (mercury), and then heated to separate the pure gold from the quicksilver. They had seen the quicksilver being mined at the New Almaden mine near San Jose. Mining technology was new and innovative, and Charles must have wanted to see it in action.

When the mine was opened, many Cornish men were recruited because of their valuable experience in draining water from underground tin mines in Cornwall. Grass Valley still has an annual Cornish Christmas and a St Piran's Day celebration, and Cornish pasties are served by restaurants in town, using recipes handed down from the original immigrant generation. Grass Valley is also twinned with the Cornish town of Bodmin. Today, there is an Empire Mine State Park in Grass Valley. There are no more mine tours, since the last mine closed in the 1950s, but as in New Almaden, there are a museum and trails marking the industrial history.

Charles and Fannie finished exploring gold mines and returned to Marysville, where Charles visited the city's Buckeye Milling Company to find out what was happening in the California grain trade. California agriculture had benefited both from the Gold Rush boom and the state's remoteness from the nation's main food-producing regions. By 1850, California agriculture was dominated by wheat and, by 1870, California was at the beginning of its "wheat bonanza" years, which lasted through the 1870s. I'm sure Charles would have shared any useful information he gleaned with his business partner and father-in-law, Edward Crosby. He also might have told him that golden opportunities were available for the grain business in California, but if so, nothing came of it, either for E. Crosby and Company or for Charles, when he left the company in 1876 to set up his own business.

I wonder if Charles and Fannie discussed the possibility of moving to California for Charles' work and to benefit his health. If so, they decided against it. Perhaps California seemed ideal for a vacation or a holiday but not as a place to live—too far from home and family, too different. Most people went west in the hope of a better life. Charles and Fannie must have thought their life in New England was right for them. After all, they were tourists, not emigrants.

They returned to Sacramento and, the following day, set off to the Calaveras Big Trees and Yosemite Valley with Mr. and Mrs. Moore, friends they had made in San Francisco. It would be the most adventurous and touristy part of their trip. Olive Logan, writing in *Galaxy Magazine* in 1870, said, "I have known Californians who went to New York, and returned home without seeing the Adirondacks; but wo betide the wandering Easterner if he seek the Pacific without bringing a trip to Yo Semite back with him!" Crofutt's guide had already recommended that travelers get *Scenes of Wonder and Curiosity in California* by J. M. Hutchings; it is quite likely that Crofutt and Hutchings knew each other, since they were both prominent in promoting travel and tourism.

The Calaveras Big Trees are a grove of giant sequoias, some up to two thousand years old. California had acquired a reputation for exaggeration, and when the trees were first brought to public attention in 1852, many thought it was just a typical tall tale. But when the truth of the amazing size of the trees was accepted, they became a tourist attraction immediately. Being in California, the modern state park offers another superlative: it's considered "the longest continuously operated tourist facility in California."

The two couples went from Sacramento to Stockton and then to Murphys, taking all day to travel eighty-five miles. They probably spent the night at the Sperry and Perry Hotel, now called Murphys Hotel and yet another of the "oldest hotels still operating" (from 1856) in California today. Mark Twain stayed there, too, and some presidents, of course. The next day they went another fifteen miles to the Big Trees, where snow had fallen, and booked into the Mammoth Grove Hotel. Built near the trees, the hotel burned down in 1943 and wasn't replaced. At that time it was no longer acceptable to build hotels so near natural wonders.

Because the Calaveras Big Trees were among the first California tourist attractions, the dominant impulse to make money initially won out over protecting the trees. Charles wrote that he saw the Original Big Tree (also called the Discovery Tree), 302 feet high and 96 feet in circumference, but for some strange reason he doesn't mention that he was actually looking at the felled tree—it had been chopped down in 1853. Five men spent twenty-two days boring into the tree with pump augers, and then driving in wedges to fell it. The bark from the tree was removed in ten-foot high sections, labeled, and taken on tour—to Woodward's Gardens in San Francisco and to New York—where it was reassembled to show the size of the original tree.

Back in the grove, the top of the felled tree's stump was smoothed off and made into a dance floor. The prostrate trunk was leveled and a saloon and a two-lane bowling alley were built on it. Another tree had its bark removed without felling it and subsequently died. I was glad to learn that the touring exhibition was roundly criticized and was a financial disaster. Author Hutchings said of the felling, "In our estimation it was a sacrilegious act" (although his moral stance may have been influenced by his business links with the hotel that catered to visitors coming to see the trees).

The pristine South Grove, with even more giant sequoia trees, was not far away, but it didn't become a tourist focus. Instead, it was sold to a lumber company and designated for logging in the early 1940s. The Calaveras Grove Association was formed to mount a difficult but ultimately successful rescue campaign. The original North Grove and the South Grove were finally united in 1967 as the Calaveras Big Trees State Park.

The natural range of the giant sequoia is a narrow band along the western slopes of the Sierra Nevada. The few remaining old growth giant sequoia groves are protected and logging is prohibited by law, but it took 150 years of challenging the lumber interests to reach this point. Ironically, more of the trees would have been felled if it hadn't been found that the brittle wood wasn't much use as lumber.

When my family went to Yosemite Valley in 1963, we drove through the Mariposa Grove of giant sequoias on the southern approach to Yosemite, and, with innocent wonder, found ourselves driving through the Wawona Tree tunnel, made in 1881. When the tree fell down in a heavy snowstorm in 1969, it was found to be 2,300 years old. I hoped the tunnel hadn't shortened its life much, but environmentalists say it was definitely why the heavy snow brought the tree down, and it could have lived much longer.

When the two couples got back to Murphys in the evening, Charles wrote that reports from Yosemite were so unfavorable that the ladies were returning to Sacramento and the men were going alone. He doesn't elaborate, so I don't know what he meant by unfavorable—was it the snow? The snow was melting. Was it the earthquake in March, whose aftershocks kept occurring in Yosemite for a couple of months? If that was worrying them, why should it be only the women who were not going? Was it the difficulty of the horseback journey? No roads yet entered the main valley from the north, so horseback was the only way in for the last sixty-five miles from the direction in which the party was traveling. Riding sidesaddle would be more arduous, but women were regularly making the journey. Fannie, a feisty woman from the tone of her forthright diaries, wouldn't have been put off. Perhaps Mrs. Moore was less robust.

For the horseback part of the journey, Charles and Mr. Moore must have reduced their luggage substantially, probably sending it back with their wives. Samuel Kneeland, a Boston doctor writing about his trip to Yosemite in 1872, advised, "A valise that can be carried by hand, or easily packed on a horse, is enough for a fortnight's trip;

for gentlemen, are desirable a broad-rimmed light hat, strong boots, serviceable but not too nice clothes, with flannel shirts; for ladies, flounces, trains, high-heeled boots, and fashionable hats are quite out of character; the clothing should be about what would be worn here in the latter part of spring; the heat may be ninety degrees F. at noon in the Valley, while the nights and mornings are cool; umbrellas are useless impediments."

The journey to their hotel in Yosemite, just under one hundred miles, took two days by stage and two by horseback. The first two days were on roads that got rougher and rougher the further they traveled. The driver on the second day, according to Charles, was "an ignorant fellow." Charles then described the area: "High mountains with little timber and much rock and chaparral. All along the large streams could be seen the ruins of the camps of the miners of 1849 and 1850." The town of Garrote, their destination for the second night, was named after the Spanish word for hanging. The town was so called because in 1849 some Mexicans were accused of stealing some gold dust and were hanged from a nearby oak tree. The locals continued to call it Garrote long after the name was changed to the more genteel Groveland in 1875.

The next morning they left Garrote, guided on horseback. According to Rev. James Buckley, writing about an earlier trip: "Some of the ladies had not been on horseback for twenty years, and some never. They were told that to ride on side-saddles is both inconvenient and dangerous, and that it is much better to ride like their husbands and brothers . . . after a brief trial, all but two or three rode like couriers, and, amid much laughter and good spirits, the cavalcade started for the Valley." What a shame Fannie wasn't there. I'm sure she would have loved it.

For Charles' party, it was a nice enough day, but the horses were in poor condition, having run wild during the winter. "One of them upon being mounted showed her natural disposition by throwing the boy and placing her feet upon his head. She was decided to be too ugly and another brought in her stead." Their horses being thin, the weather warm, and the riders not hardened to the saddle, they only made about ten miles by noon and were still high above the Merced

River in the Yosemite Valley as darkness approached. They carried on, leading their horses down the steep mountainside, and reached the bottom, where they startled four deer, after it was quite dark. Finally they reached McCann's House, an Irish whiskey shop, and slept. They had traveled thirty-five miles by horse.

The next day was hot and clear, and at 7 A.M. they got on their horses again to finish the journey up the Merced River valley, passing Mr. Hutchings taking a group out. Their hotel, opposite Yosemite Falls, was probably the one owned by Mr. Hutchings, who seemed to have his hand in all the local ventures. Charles' diary was hastily scribbled and sounded breathless, listing all the amazing sights they had seen: "On our right was Bridal Veil Fall, beautiful indeed upon the left and looming up before us was El Capitan down its abrupt side fell a beautiful white mist, near it housed the Virgin Fall . . . On the right Cathedral Rocks and Spires the Three Graces and Sentinel Rock and Glacier Point were to be seen and beyond South Dome which from our stand point resembled a half dome. On the left the Three Brothers, Eagle Point, Yosemite Fall, and North Dome were to be seen."

The next day they toured the valley on horseback, visiting Mirror Lake—"the reflections were good"—and then Lower Yosemite Falls—"got drenched in the spray." After dinner, they climbed up to Sentinel Rock to see the mountains stretching to the horizon all around. Their attempt to see everything they possibly could in their short visit reminded me of Americans who try to "do Europe" in impossibly brief time frames.

On Sunday, Charles must have found it strange not to be going to the church services that he so rarely missed. They rode on horseback to the upper end of the valley to see more waterfalls and an impressive granite dome, but "remained quiet during the afternoon." As a man of his times, Charles was probably influenced by the prevalent nineteenth-century Romanticism; visiting wild and awesome landscapes was considered a way to get close to God. Perhaps he imagined Yosemite as his cathedral, reflecting on the scenes of God's amazing power while he rested in preparation for the next day of hard riding to get back out of the valley.

When my family visited Yosemite in 1963, we were equally

impressed by the vast, dazzling, perpendicular granite rock faces and the waterfalls seeming to fall endlessly, but the number of visitors had increased dramatically since 1872. In one of his columns sent back to the *Brattleboro Reformer*, my father wrote, "After some 90 miles of uphill mountain grind, with the little trailer feeling bigger by the mile, we arrived at what I call a madhouse of trailers and tents—some 500 of them in Camp 7 at Yosemite. I grouched about 'too many damn people' and Mary Ann suggested I look above the people at the most amazing rise of granite wall we have ever seen, and falls spurting in every direction! After a cold dip in the Merced River (which comes out of one of those falls) I felt fairly human and had a good sleep as the 2,000th sardine in this over-camped campsite." The number of visitors in 1963 was close to two million. (It is now about four million, but most visitors arrive by shuttle buses, and campers must have reservations, which sell out months in advance.)

John Muir, the naturalist and writer who was later to become one of the founders of the American environmental movement, was living nearby, in Yosemite, when Charles was there. The epicenter of the strong earthquake that Charles had noted a few weeks earlier was about 150 miles south of Yosemite Valley, and struck while Muir was sleeping in the cabin he had built beneath Sentinel Rock. In a letter to a friend, he wrote, "We have had a glorious storm of the kind called earthquake. I've just been writing an account of it for the *New York Tribune*. It would seem strange that any portion of our perpendicular walls are left unshattered. It is delightful to be trotted and dumpled on our Mother's mountain knee. I hope we will be blessed with some more. The first shock of the morning at half-past two o'clock was the most sublime storm I ever experienced. Though I had never enjoyed a storm of this sort, the thrilling motion could not be mistaken, and I ran out of my cabin, both glad and frightened, shouting, 'A noble earthquake!' feeling sure I was going to learn something."

He went on to describe the same Yosemite springtime that Charles saw. "Since March 26th, we have enjoyed, on the average, about a dozen shocks per day . . . These forty days of earthquake ague have made no visible alteration to the health of the valley. Now is the birth-time of leaves; the pines are retassled, and the oaks are sprayed with young purple. Spring is fully committed. Ferns are a foot high, willows are letting fly drifts of ripe seeds. Balm of Gilead poplars, after weeks of caution, have launched their buds full of red and leaves of tender glossy yellow. Cherries, honeysuckles, violets, bluets, buttercups, larkspurs, gilias, are full of bloom of leaf and flower." I wouldn't be surprised if the faded flowers I found pressed between pages in Charles' diary came from Yosemite that spring.

John Muir and Charles were both thirty-three years old, but I doubt they would have found much else in common. Muir, who was born in Scotland and emigrated to Wisconsin with his family as a child, had gone to Canada during the Civil War in 1863 to avoid the draft, unlike Charles who had volunteered to fight. He was clever but unconventional, and worked as a sawyer and carpenter to fund his time spent studying nature in Yosemite. He initially worked for Mr. Hutchings, designing and building a sawmill that ran on water power from Yosemite Falls. He refused on principle to cut down living trees, but was willing to saw into boards a quantity of pine trees that had blown down in a big storm. I wasn't surprised to learn that he eventually fell out with Hutchings and built a cabin to live in, spending winters in Black's Hotel.

It was Muir who persuaded President Teddy Roosevelt to make Yosemite a National Park in 1906. Ownership of Yosemite had been transferred to the State of California in 1864, but Muir became unhappy with the state's supervision. It allowed road tunnels to be bored through trees, meadows to be converted into hayfields and pastures, and the mountain ramparts above the valley to be shorn by sheep and logged by lumbermen.

When I realized that humans are seriously misusing the planet, Muir became one of my heroes. I didn't have enough time to follow Charles' route into Yosemite, so I decided to pay homage to Muir by cycling eight miles, north of San Francisco, to Muir Woods National Monument, with its canyon of ancient redwoods and its important place in the history of the American conservation movement. It seemed especially appropriate, as it was celebrating its one-hundredth anniversary.

From the hostel, I cycled west along the car-free bay shoreline and across the Golden Gate Bridge on the sidewalk for bikes and walkers, stopping to enjoy the view of the landmark bridge above me and the unusual view of the city from the bay. The first design for the bridge, which was built in the 1930s, was said to look like "an upside-down rat trap," so we are fortunate that they chose a simple, classic design instead, and the glowing dark orange color that was the primer became the perfect color for the final coat.

Beyond the bridge I continued to Sausalito, which in 1871 was a nascent town that Charles and Fannie visited one day by ferry. (The ferry from San Francisco was started by a group of developers who owned land in Sausalito and were keen to show it to buyers and tourists.) As usual, I hadn't been able to buy a map with contours, so I found out the hard way that, from Sausalito, I had to cycle up one thousand feet in elevation on Route 1, where I joined the Panoramic Highway along a high, open ridgetop. It was two lanes with a small shoulder, few cars, and no large vehicles. When I reached a spot with a good overlook, I stopped to enjoy the magnificent views all around: northeast toward Napa Valley, east to the Sierra Coastal Range, south back to the Bay Area, and west out to the broad Pacific. It made the hard climb well worth the effort, but I was thankful for Bike Friday's twenty-seven gears.

After cycling along the Panoramic Highway for a few miles, I turned down the west side of the ridge into the secluded and atmospheric Redwood Canyon, its old-growth redwoods soaring sublimely into the sky on the southern flank of Mount Tamalpais. I've said I like trees, but I get really emotional about ancient trees. I enjoy checking out old yews in Britain, often associated with churchyards and predating Christianity. A yew said to be over two thousand years old, with a girth of thirty-two feet, is in a churchyard seven miles from my home and marks what was a sacred site in pre-Christian times.

The peaceful Coast Miwok Indians living along the Marin Peninsula believed that all beings, including plants and animals, possessed a spiritual essence, so they venerated the redwoods. The nineteenth-century newcomers saw only valuable timber for making things.

I find myself attracted to Indian spirituality because their relationship to the earth seems to match my outlook, but I know their beliefs are so bound up in their own cultures and places that it makes no sense for me to adopt those beliefs. Perhaps it is more about teasing out some of the universal principles within. When I was reading about the "sense of place" in relation to Robert Frost, I found an illuminating analysis of indigenous notions of place by Jeff Malpas, an Australian philosopher: "Indigenous conceptions of place assert an essential belonging of human beings to the places they inhabit . . . Place is formed through . . . an active engagement with place and places . . . " He contrasts this with "ownership," which is so important in our culture and which implies that we can claim authority over a place and exclude others from it. "Place has to be understood as itself a dynamic and relational structure in which we are already embedded, rather than some static object over which 'ownership' can simply be asserted." This is an aspect of indigenous spirituality that I can make my own: trying to shift from my human-centered worldview to a more earth-centered one. It occurred to me why I had so readily believed that the Abenakis passed through Vermont but didn't live there—failing to understand that their "passing through" was really about traveling around the several places where they needed to live throughout the year to obtain food for themselves.

The coast redwood is unique to a narrow strip near the coast in middle and northern California, related to the giant sequoia but a different species. All but 4 percent of the old-growth redwoods were logged in the nineteenth and early twentieth centuries, so we can consider ourselves lucky that Muir Woods was saved. Watching the indiscriminate logging near Napa Valley in 1887, Robert Louis Stevenson wrote, "Redwoods and redskins, the two noblest indigenous living things, alike condemned." What saved Muir Woods from logging? Here's the timeline:

The Coast Miwoks, decimated by disease to 10 percent of their original population, were so few in number that Spaniards claimed their land. In 1836, the Mexican government granted a large tract to William Antonio Richardson, who had married into a Californio family and taken Mexican nationality. After some years of using the land for grazing and logging, he sold it to Samuel Throckmorton, who farmed and logged, but kept a large area around Redwood Canyon as his hunting preserve. After his death, his daughter sold it to the Tamalpais Land and Water Company to pay off her father's debts. The company granted the hunting preserve to the Tamalpais Sportsman's Association.

By the turn of the century development pressures were increasing, and a proposal was made to dam Redwood Creek. One of the members of the Sportsman's Association was William Kent, a wealthy resident with conservation leanings. He bought 612 acres to keep the redwoods safe, supported by his wife Elizabeth, who was an ardent conservationist. A few years later, the North Coast Water Company tried to appropriate part of the land to build a reservoir for San Francisco. John Muir suggested to the Kents a way to circumvent this threat—giving the land to the federal government—and in 1908, President Theodore Roosevelt declared it a National Monument under the recently passed Antiquities Act.

The Muir Woods Visitor Center was almost deserted on a September weekday morning. I paid to enter, locked up my bike, and walked along a path into the towering woods with no one else in sight. I stopped and looked up, higher and higher and even higher, up to the very top of the trees. Sunlight and shadows rippled down the tall trunks and silvery dust motes danced in the air. The trees I was looking at were so venerable and old, anywhere from 500 to 1,200 years old, that they made me feel humble. The beauty and the silence prompted me to wonder. Perhaps I'm one of those people who find spirituality through nature rather than religion, and through nature I can nourish my soul.

But I worried about the future. Can we humans rein in our destructive urges to want more, more, more before it's too late? Can we stop our rush to the climate-warming Armageddon and choose a more sustainable route? I tried to calm my pessimistic side and buoy up my hope and optimism. All I could do was to make a resolution: keep trying, have faith in human possibilities, recognize that I can't do it alone or all the time . . .

I left Muir Woods with my new resolve, cycling down through the stately trees to wild and rocky Muir Beach on the Pacific, where I felt very small looking out at the distant horizon past the sand and surf.

*A photograph can't do justice to the height
and grandeur of the redwood trees.*

Then I rejoined Route 1, called the Shoreline Highway here, to get back up to the high ridge above and back to San Francisco. I had paid homage to John Muir, but more importantly, I had experienced a special place of extraordinary beauty, and I had communed with some of Earth's ancient denizens.

When Charles was in Yosemite, I wish he had come across a friend of John Muir's called Galen Clark. Clark ran a hotel at the southern entrance to Yosemite and, when Congress granted Yosemite to the State of California in 1864, he was made a commissioner and subsequently a Guardian of the Valley. If Charles had met him, Clark might have told him that living in Yosemite had saved his life. In 1853, at the age of thirty-nine, he had contracted a lung infection, diagnosed as consumption. Doctors gave him six months to live, but counseled rest and outdoor air. He moved to the hills near Yosemite to run a hotel, regained his health, and lived till he was ninety-six. Perhaps Charles would have remembered Galen and considered moving to Yosemite when he was diagnosed with consumption five years later.

On the fifth day of their visit to Yosemite, Charles, Mr. Moore, and their guide, Tom Edwards, were in the saddle at 6 A.M. to start the journey back out. They rode their horses for seventeen and a half hours and sixty-five miles, arriving in Garrote at 11.30 P.M. Charles wrote, "Said to have been the quickest ride ever made from the valley via that route." I'm impressed that my great-grandfather managed such a feat.

There was no stage the next day, so the two men panned for gold in a stream near Garrote and obtained a few specks. In the evening they watched "a dance by 500 Indians in a ring." The Miwok Indians living in the area—continuing to harvest acorns, fish, and game—apparently got on reasonably well with settlers, but I'm sure there wasn't a large enough population to find five hundred people for dancing. Charles perhaps exaggerated the number, but I read that groups of Miwok would travel far to visit local friends in this area and "would sometimes put on a fandango dressed in their native garb, during which they jumped up and down, not forgetting to pass a hat afterwards." Perhaps that is what Charles and Mr. Moore happened upon.

The next day they left Garrote at five A.M. and started the long journey to rejoin their wives and board the first of the trains that would take them back to their homes in the East. They must have been exhausted after all the horseback riding, stage journeys, and the train not arriving until well after midnight. In his diary, Charles made desultory notes across Nevada, Utah, Wyoming, and Colorado; described a beautiful sunset in the Rocky Mountains; and then stopped recording altogether in Kansas City.

I started my journey home from Los Angeles on Amtrak's Southwest Chief. I performed my trick of sleeping comfortably in the Observation Lounge car and set my alarm for 5.30 A.M, so I could have a look as we went by La Posada, the Arizona hotel where I had remembered my great-grandparents' 1871 train trip and started this journey. La Posada (The Resting Place) was built by the Santa Fe Railway in 1929, long after the Rices' trip. It was one of the last great railroad hotels. The design, by the renowned architect Mary Colter, drew on her vision of a wealthy Spanish landowner's grand hacienda. It was "fantasy heritage," as I had discovered in Santa Barbara—but the handsome, newly restored hotel, with the striking russet curves of its clay-tiled roof, contrasting cream-painted adobe walls, and wide covered arcades set the scene for me to imagine the train stopping in the 1870s, with pioneer tourists like my great-grandparents.

Their trip was definitely the trip of a lifetime. They could have returned home any time, but were clearly determined to see as much as possible in this newly accessible part of the country. Traveling in those days was much less comfortable than it is now, but new sights and new experiences must have been more important to them than comfort, as long as they also had some interludes for recovery.

As soon as they were home, it was back to their lives of hard work and church duties for several more years, then the big move away from Brattleboro and the subsequent births of Howard and then Marion. Charles' failing health after he made the big break with his father-in-law must have been terrifying, but I have a feeling that the farm manager job at Talladega College gave him some personal satisfaction. I hope so. I wish I had known all of this before my grandfather died so I could have talked about it with him.

I also would have liked to talk with my grandfather and my uncle about whether Charles died of his war wounds. Our family has always thought so. When I was trying to find out why they went out West, I looked for evidence that the trip was to benefit his health. In his diaries after the Civil War, he mentioned his war wound acting up occasionally, but he definitely didn't appear to be in bad health. He worked long hours and was often away from home for days at a time on business. He regularly went on trips and holidays with Fannie and had many responsibilities at church. His marathon journey by horseback out of the Yosemite Valley surely belies the notion of chronic ill health. Then I found a relevant family document. When he was medically discharged from the army, Charles received a small War Pension. After his death, Fannie applied for a War Widow's Pension. To be eligible, Charles must have died of his war injuries. One of the affidavits supporting her application was written by a long-time friend of Charles, who wrote: "In the fall of 1871 . . . he was in a very bad state of health and his wound gave him trouble and he went with his wife to California and spent the winter for the benefit of his health . . ." So, I thought, the friend exaggerated to help Fannie—and his statement is in the family records that my uncle kept, becoming the origin of another family myth.

I have been struck by the fact that money did so little to protect that fairly recent generation from so much illness, death, and loss. Through their diaries, I've grown very fond of both of them. During the eight years when he had TB, Charles never gave up. He kept on rising to new challenges. Although his diaries don't exactly sing, they reveal his quiet courage in volunteering to fight for his country, respecting the Chinese when they were being vilified, and attending a black church in the post–Civil War segregationist South. Fannie was also courageous, determined to do the best for her children, her family, and others in need, and she had that feisty, edgy side that I liked.

———

A FTER LEAVING La Posada, the Southwest Chief continued through Arizona and New Mexico, historically Spanish and Mexican until annexed by the United States in 1848. These dry, mesa-studded states show constant evidence of the millennia of occupation by Indians, then Hispanics and Europeans. I remembered our eye-opening climb up footholds carved in the stone to the vibrant Indian community of Acoma Pueblo during our 1963 road trip on Route 66.

We stopped at Albuquerque station for an "extended Amtrak break," which enabled two women in hard hats and long-handled sponges to wash all the windows on the long train. The Amtrak Station was new, but reminiscent of the original station's Mission Revival style, a welcome improvement over a pathetic Amshack. I strolled along the platform and bought some woven coasters from an Indian, possibly a Navajo. When I looked at them later, I found a label saying "Made in India." I chuckled, and wondered if American Indians are outsourcing their manufacturing to the Asian Indians in this globalized world.

Back on the train, slowly climbing away from Albuquerque through more Indian pueblo country and into the foothills of the Rockies, I found myself considering what I had gained from this trip. I felt a much stronger connection with Charles and Fannie. If it weren't for them, I wouldn't have undertaken this train journey, which is a legacy for which I am immensely grateful.

I've learned much more about the settlement of the West, and the West as it is today. My earlier naïve and simplistic picture has been transformed, leaving me with a much better understanding of the nineteenth-century Western frontier—why its allure beckoned to so many and captured the imaginations of my great-grandparents and then me. I've also learned how Western history-telling keeps changing as it gets rewritten from present-day perspectives, as does Wild West storytelling. The prominence of the storytelling when I was growing up was a particular feature of those times. It has diminished, but not disappeared, over the years, and the Wild West is still an enduring vision for many.

I've also learned more about myself, becoming aware of the need for a new inner framework for living in this scary, unpredictable world: one that fits with science but acknowledges, at a deeper level, that there are other ways of knowing, and that moves away from our human-centered focus to a focus on the centrality of the Earth and the universe. I have countless more philosophical and spiritual avenues to explore.

As the train passed more pueblo communities, I reflected on the incredible diversity of the American people. Prejudice and conflict continue, but I hope that my outlook of inclusiveness, based on a family legacy of concern for the wider community, will prevail. I am thankful that the American Indians didn't disappear as foretold, but were resilient and survived with their identities still mostly intact.

I hope they keep developing their cultural relationship to the Earth and perhaps help the rest of us to renegotiate ours.

We headed northeast through the rugged and beautiful Rocky Mountains in northern New Mexico and into Colorado. At Glorieta Pass, we were more than seven thousand feet above sea level. As I was observing the magnificent mountain views from the Observation Lounge car, the man in the next seat turned to me with a question. "Do you know about the 1862 Civil War battle at Glorieta Pass?" I said I had no idea the war had even been fought that far west. He told me, "The Confederates took the pass, hoping to take Colorado and then California on their way to taking the valuable gold and silver mines. Then the Unionists came up from the rear and destroyed their supply wagons, forcing the Confederates to retreat. We now know that the strategic importance of stopping the Confederates here was equivalent to Gettysburg and Antietam." I thanked him for passing on an unusual story about the Civil War. Then he listened while I told him all about my great-grandfather at the First Battle of Bull Run.

I turned to look out the wide window as our train rolled along through the high desert below the Sangre de Cristo Mountains, where the dark green junipers and pinyons stood out against the sun-crimsoned sandstone crags and the sky began to redden. Like my great-grandparents, I was leaving the Rocky Mountains at sunset to return home.

# ACKNOWLEDGMENTS

I THANK MY FAMILY: my parents John and Marion Hooper who encouraged my love of travel, exploration, and writing about it; my Uncle Howard who got me hooked on family history; my brothers Steve and John who helped with family stories and photos; my sister-in-law Jackie Hooper, my son Eric Hildrew, and his wife Sarah Cockburn who all commented on early drafts.

I'd also like to thank the Arvon Foundation whose stimulating creative nonfiction writing course I took in 2012. It led me to Carole Angier, the incisive tutor who gave me the confidence to write this book, and her colleague, Simon Rae, who showed me the value of constructive criticism, which made the book better without in any way detracting from it being my book.

Many friends are also due thanks for their helpful comments on the book, especially Moira Knowles, Edna Fletcher, Ruth Hetherington, and Margaret Brittin. Polly Pettit suggested I read her favorite novel about the West, Wallace Stegner's *Angle of Repose* (1971), which had a big influence on my own thinking about the history of the region.

I am also indebted to the World Wide Web. I don't think this book would have come to fruition without the internet-enabled access I had to people and to information, ranging from nineteenth-century newspapers, letters, and books to Google Maps and Street View.

And finally, my heartfelt thanks to Justin Race at the University of Nevada Press, for his support and encouragement, and for his willingness to take a chance on my first book.

# ABOUT THE AUTHOR

MARY ANN HOOPER was born in March 1944 and grew up in Brattleboro, Vermont. She received a Harvard degree, fell in love with rock climbing and a British classmate, and moved to London. There she worked for an advertising trade magazine, a North London weekly, and a daily newspaper in Milton Keynes, outside of the city. She went on to become a social worker and social services manager for thirty-five years.

Hooper now lives in the small town of Wirksworth, near the British Peak District, where she can occasionally visit her son and his family in Edinburgh. She is helping to set up a community land trust for building low-energy-cost housing for local families, and she helps manage the town website, www.gowirksworth.com. She has been writing this book for the last ten years.